tempt

tempt

Decadent and delicious
chocolate recipes

This edition published by Parragon Books Ltd in 2015 and distributed by

Parragon Inc.
440 Park Avenue South, 13th Floor
New York, NY 10016
www.parragon.com/lovefood

LOVE FOOD is an imprint of Parragon Books Ltd

ISBN 978-1-4723-9261-9

Printed in China

New recipes by Mima Sinclair
New photography by Mike Cooper
New home economy by Lincoln Jefferson
Introduction and incidental text by Christine McFadden
Designed by Bethan Kalynka

Notes for the Reader
This book uses standard kitchen measuring spoons and cups. All spoon and cup measurements are level unless otherwise indicated. Unless otherwise stated, milk is assumed to be whole, eggs are large, individual vegetables are medium, and pepper is freshly ground black pepper. Unless otherwise stated, all root vegetables should be peeled prior to using.

The times given are only an approximate guide. Preparation times differ according to the techniques used by different people and the cooking times may also vary from those given.

CONTENTS

FOOD OF THE GODS

Most of us probably don't realize that chocolate, one of the most loved and addictive confections of all, comes from the fruit of the cacao tree, or *Theobroma cacao*, from the Greek, meaning "food of the gods."

Most of us also think of chocolate as a solid substance; however, for much of its long history, it was enjoyed as a beverage instead of as something to be eaten.

So how and when did this transformation from bean to beverage to bar take place?

From bean to beverage

In the early 1500s, the explorer Christopher Columbus discovered cacao beans in Central America while searching for a route to the spice islands in the East. The native Aztecs thought the beans had magical powers and even used them as a kind of primitive currency. The story goes that they bartered a sack of their precious beans for some of Columbus's merchandise. They also offered him their special drink made from crushed beans laced with chiles and cornmeal. Unaware of the their future economic worth, Columbus took some beans to Spain, more out of curiosity than because he enjoyed the unpalatable drink.

Moving on about twenty years, the Spanish conquistador Hernando Cortés arrived on the scene. Unlike Columbus, he quickly caught on to the bean's enormous potential, and he, too, took beans back to Spain, along with a recipe for *xocolatl*, the Aztecs' chocolate drink. Just as he predicted, the beverage became fashionable among the wealthy cognoscenti. Meanwhile, the Spanish conquistadors made their fortunes by establishing cacao plantations in Central America and elsewhere. For them, money really did grow on trees.

Chocolate travels the world

In 1580, Spain became home to the first chocolate-processing plant. From then on there was no holding it back. The passion for chocolate-drinking spread like wildfire through Europe, and eventually to North America and the rest of the world.

Sugar and spice

By the late sixteenth century, chocolate manufacturing had become more sophisticated, and the drink was certainly more palatable. Sugar, a novel ingredient at the time, and fragrant spices—cinnamon, vanilla, and musk, for example—were added to the roasted ground beans. The mix was ground again to a fine paste, which, in turn, was molded into chunky blocks. The blocks were used for making a drink, just as they are in Spain and Mexico today.

From beverage to bar

As the early chocolate-makers discovered, cacao contains cacao butter, which produced unappetizing fatty globules on the surface of the drink. Eventually, a Dutch chemist figured out a way of separating the cacao butter and he invented a hydraulic press that successfully dealt with the problem.

But now there was a new dilemma: what to do with all that valuable cacao butter? Yet again, a solution was found; the melted cacao butter was mixed with ground cacao beans and sugar to make a smooth paste that was liquid enough to pour into a mold. It was from this novel idea that "eating chocolate" was developed.

GROWING, HARVESTING,
and Processing

The cacao tree grows only in tropical regions 10 degrees either side of the equator. The Ivory Coast, Ghana, and Indonesia are the world's largest producers, followed by Cameroon, Nigeria, Brazil, Ecuador, the Dominican Republic, Malaysia, and Togo.

The pointed fruit or pods sprout directly from the tree's trunk and branches. About 8 inches long, they come in gloriously flamboyant colors: bright green, red, purple, yellow, and gold—the hue changes as they ripen. Inside the pod are the precious beans, nestling in a cocoon of sweetish white pulp.

Bean varieties and flavors

There are three main types of beans:

Criollo: Now almost extinct, this is the finest, most expensive, most sought-after cacao. It has an exceptional flavor and aroma.

Forastero: Making up most of the world's production, this is a hardy variety with robust flavors. More bitter than Criollo, it's used mainly for blending with other beans.

Trinitario: Bred in Trinidad in the eighteenth century, this is a hybrid of Criollo and Forastero. The flavor combines the robustness of Forastero and the delicacy of Criollo.

Processing

The transformation from plump pods to deluxe chocolate is one that draws equally on the skills of both the grower and the chocolate-maker.

The process begins when the ripe pods are harvested. They are cut from the trees, then left to rest for a week to ten days before the husks are split in two and the beans and surrounding pulp are scooped out.

Next comes the all-important fermentation—this is crucial for developing the final flavor and aroma of the chocolate. The beans and pulp are piled in a wooden box or on banana leaves, covered, and left for six to seven days while microorganisms do their work. As the beans ferment, they darken, and the wonderful aroma of cocoa begins to emerge.

The beans are dried in the sun for up to two weeks. They are then ready to be shoveled into sacks and shipped across the world to the chocolate manufacturers, where the transformation continues.

Roasting

When they arrive at the factory, the beans are cleaned, graded, and then roasted. A crucial part of the process, roasting develops the flavor and enriches the color of the bean. It's vital to get it right, otherwise the flavor will be ruined.

Grinding

The roasted beans are passed through a winnowing machine that blows off the outer shell. The nibs—the edible heart of the bean—are then ground between metal rollers, producing a liquid paste called cocoa mass or liquor. This consists of about 45 percent cocoa solids and 55 percent cocoa butter—a unique fat that is solid at room temperature but miraculously melts in the mouth.

Conching

To create the velvety-smooth chocolate we love, the liquid chocolate is gently heated and stirred in a conching machine. This, in turn, fine-tunes the texture and flavor. Cheap chocolate is conched for as little as 12 hours, while top-quality chocolate is conched for up to a week.

Tempering

The final step in the process, tempering involves heating and cooling the chocolate to precise temperatures. This produces top-notch chocolate with a gorgeous sheen, great texture, and a good, sharp snap.

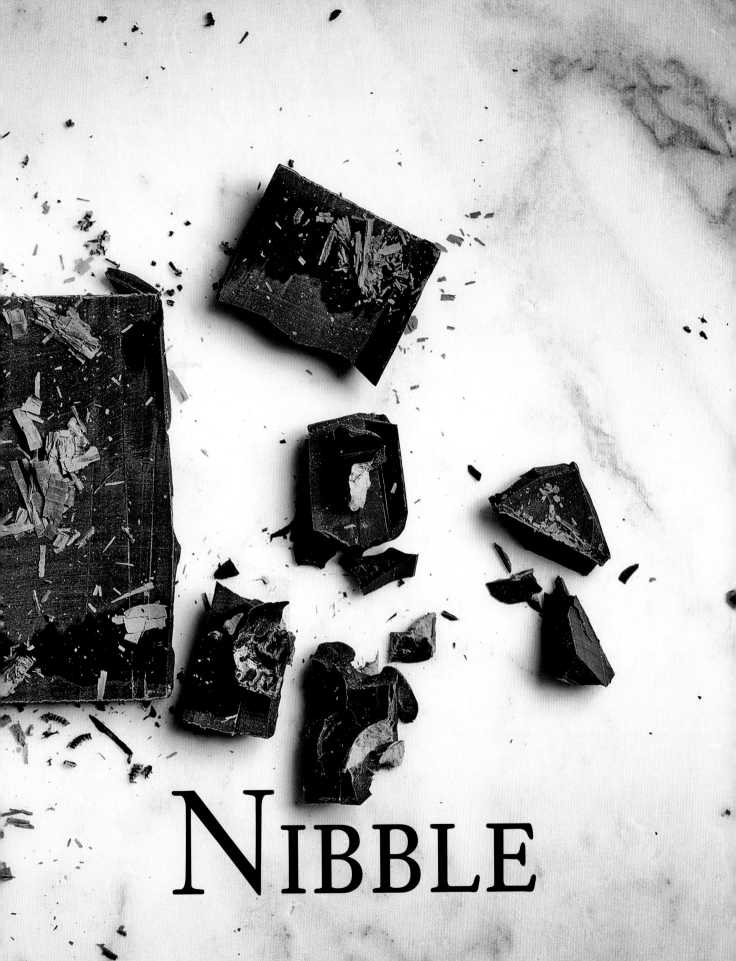

NIBBLE

CHOCOLATE PRETZEL
Fudge Squares

Makes 16

These are so easy to make. The salty pretzels counteract the rich sweetness of the chocolate and condensed milk.

Prep: 15 mins   Cook: 8–10 mins, plus setting

Ingredients

26 mini pretzels
(about 6 ounces)

1 tablespoon sunflower oil,
for oiling

2 tablespoons unsalted butter,
diced

1¾ cups milk chocolate chips

1 (14-ounce) can sweetened
condensed milk

1 teaspoon vanilla extract

1. Coarsely chop 10 of the pretzels.

2. Lightly brush a 10-inch square baking pan with the oil and line it with nonstick parchment paper, snipping diagonally into the corners, then pressing the paper into the pan so that the bottom and sides are lined. There should be a 2-inch overhang on all sides.

3. Put the butter, chocolate chips, condensed milk, and vanilla extract into a heatproof bowl set over a saucepan of gently simmering water and heat, stirring occasionally, for 8–10 minutes, or until the chocolate has just melted and the mixture is smooth and warm but not hot. Remove from the heat and stir in the chopped pretzels.

4. Pour the mixture into the prepared pan, smooth the surface with a spatula, and push in the whole pretzels. Let cool for 1 hour. Cover with plastic wrap, then chill in the refrigerator for 1–2 hours, or until firm.

5. Lift the fudge out of the pan, peel off the paper, and cut it into 16 squares. Store in an airtight container in a cool, dry place for up to 2 weeks.

WHITE CHOCOLATE
Rocky Road

Makes 20

When cooking with white chocolate, use a brand that contains cocoa butter. White chocolate has a delicate structure and the cocoa butter helps it withstand heating.

Prep: 30 mins, plus chilling   Cook: 10 mins

Ingredients

7 ounces white chocolate

5 tablespoons butter

8 shortbread cookies

¼ cup mini pink and white marshmallows

½ cup halved candied cherries

1 tablespoon freeze-dried raspberries

1. Line an 8-inch square cake pan with parchment paper.

2. Break the chocolate into small pieces and cut the butter into cubes. Put both into a heatproof bowl set over a saucepan of gently simmering water and heat until melted.

3. Put the cookies into a plastic bag, seal the bag, and gently crush the cookies with a rolling pin to make small pieces. Add them to the melted chocolate mixture, then stir in the marshmallows and two-thirds of the cherries.

4. Spoon the batter into the pan, spreading evenly. Place the remaining cherries on the surface and sprinkle with the raspberries.

5. Let set in a cool place for about 1 hour.

6. Cut into 20 squares and serve.

NUTTY CHOCOLATE Puddles

Makes 24–30

Chocolate puddles are adult chocolate disks and you won't meet anyone who wouldn't gladly receive a little box of these.

Prep: 20 mins, plus cooling and setting   Cook: 10 mins

Ingredients

1–1½ tablespoons each pistachio nuts, almonds, hazelnuts, and macadamia nuts

4 ounces semisweet chocolate, finely chopped

4 ounces milk chocolate, finely chopped

4 ounces white chocolate, finely chopped

1. Preheat the oven to 400°F. Spread the nuts over a large baking sheet and roast in the preheated oven for 5–6 minutes, until golden. Coarsely chop into small pieces and let cool.

2. Put the semisweet chocolate, milk chocolate, and white chocolate into separate heatproof bowls set over saucepans of gently simmering water and heat until melted. Remove from the heat and let cool for 1–2 minutes.

3. Spoon generous teaspoons of the chocolate onto wax paper to make 8–10 puddles of each type of chocolate. Sprinkle with the chopped nuts and let cool and set firm.

4. Carefully remove the set puddles from the paper. Store in an airtight container in a cool place, but not in the refrigerator, for up to 2 weeks.

VARIATION
Try adding finely chopped dried fruit, such as sour cherries or crystallized ginger, to the nut mix; or you could swirl the different chocolates together in one puddle.

SALTED CARAMEL &
Chocolate Bites

Sea salt and caramel form one of the most perfect combinations, enhanced here by the addition of crunchy walnuts.

Prep: 30 mins   Cook: 35–40 mins

Ingredients

1 tablespoon sunflower oil, for oiling

7 ounces semisweet chocolate, coarsely chopped

1¼ sticks unsalted butter

2 eggs

¾ cup firmly packed light brown sugar

⅓ cup all-purpose flour

1 teaspoon baking powder

½ cup coarsely chopped walnuts

⅓ cup dulce de leche (caramel sauce)

1 tablespoon sea salt

1. Preheat the oven to 325°F. Lightly brush an 8-inch square baking pan with oil. Line it with nonstick parchment paper, snipping diagonally into the corners, then pressing the paper into the pan so that the bottom and sides are lined.

2. Put 2½ ounces of the chocolate and all the butter into a heatproof bowl, set the bowl over a saucepan of gently simmering water, and heat, stirring occasionally, until melted.

3. Put the eggs and sugar into a mixing bowl, then sift in the flour and baking powder. Stir in the melted chocolate mixture and beat together until blended. Add the walnuts and remaining chocolate and stir together. Pour the batter into the prepared pan and smooth the surface using a spatula.

4. Put the dulce de leche into a small mixing bowl and beat, then swirl it through the chocolate mixture, using a fork. Sprinkle with the sea salt and bake in the preheated oven for 30–35 minutes, or until the cake begins to shrink slightly from the sides of the pan. Let cool in the pan for 1 hour.

5. Lift the cake out of the pan, peel off the paper, and cut it into 20 squares. Store in an airtight container in a cool, dry place for up to 2 days.

Nibble

CHOCOLATE ORANGE
Cannoli

Makes 20–24

One of chocolate's most natural pairing ingredients is orange. In this recipe, the oil in the grated orange zest brings out the bittersweet flavor of the chocolate.

Prep: 40 mins, plus chilling   Cook: 25 mins

Ingredients

1 egg

2 tablespoons medium red wine

1⅓ cups all-purpose flour

2 teaspoons granulated sugar

pinch of salt

1 tablespoon all-purpose flour, for dusting

1 tablespoon sunflower oil, for brushing

sunflower oil, for deep-frying

1 tablespoon confectioners' sugar, to decorate

Chocolate & Orange Filling

3 cups ricotta cheese

2 tablespoons brandy

2 teaspoons vanilla extract

2 tablespoons unsweetened cocoa powder

3 tablespoons confectioners' sugar

¼ cup chopped candied oranges

3 tablespoons chopped semisweet chocolate

finely grated zest of 2 large oranges

pinch of ground cinnamon

1. Beat the egg and red wine together. Put the flour, granulated sugar, and salt into a food processor and blend. With the motor running, slowly pour in the egg mixture until the ingredients just come together to form a dough. Turn out the dough onto a lightly floured work surface and knead. Roll into a ball, wrap in plastic wrap, and chill in the refrigerator for at least 1 hour.

2. Meanwhile, to make the filling, beat together the cheese, brandy, and vanilla extract until creamy. Sift in the cocoa powder and confectioners' sugar and stir in the candied oranges, chocolate, orange zest, and cinnamon. Cover and chill until required.

3. Cut the dough into four equal pieces. Use a pasta machine to roll one piece into a strip about 20 inches long, or roll out on a lightly floured work surface until the dough is thin enough to see through. Cut out 1½-inch squares. Brush some cannoli tubes with oil and diagonally roll a piece of dough around each. Use a dab of water to seal the corners where they meet and press firmly.

4. Heat enough oil for deep-frying to 350–375°F, or until a cube of bread browns in 30 seconds. Add 2–3 cannoli tubes at a time to the oil and fry until the pastry is golden brown and crisp. Use a slotted spoon to remove the tubes and transfer to paper towels to drain. Continue until all the dough has been used, gently sliding the shells off the tubes, and applying oil before using again.

5. Store in an airtight container for up to 3 days until required. Just before serving, use a pastry bag or a spoon to fill the tubes from both ends. If you fill the cannoli in advance, they will become soggy. Dust with confectioners' sugar and serve immediately.

ESPRESSO
Truffles

Makes 12

For a different twist on these luscious coffee truffles, simply replace the coffee with Irish cream liqueur or any orange-flavored liqueur such as triple sec.

Prep: 40 mins   Cook: 5–10 mins, plus chilling

Ingredients

10½ ounces semisweet chocolate, coarsely chopped

2 tablespoons heavy cream

1 tablespoon strong espresso coffee, cooled

2 tablespoons coffee liqueur

4 tablespoons unsalted butter, softened and diced

edible gold leaf, to decorate (optional)

1. Put 3½ ounces of the chocolate and all the cream into a heatproof bowl set over a saucepan of gently simmering water and heat until the chocolate is melted.

2. Remove from the heat, add the coffee, coffee liqueur, and butter, and whisk for 3–4 minutes, or until thickened. Transfer to an airtight container and chill in the refrigerator for 6–8 hours, or until firm.

3. Line a baking sheet with nonstick parchment paper. Scoop teaspoonfuls of the mixture and, using the palms of your hands, roll them into truffle-size balls. Place the balls on the prepared baking sheet, cover with plastic wrap, and freeze for 6–8 hours.

4. Put the remaining chocolate into a heatproof bowl, set the bowl over a saucepan of gently simmering water, and heat until melted. Using two forks, dip each truffle into the chocolate to coat evenly. Return them to the prepared baking sheet and chill in the refrigerator for 1–2 hours, or until firm.

5. Decorate each truffle with edible gold leaf, if using. Store in an airtight container in the refrigerator for up to 5 days.

CHOCOLATE COOKIE
Dough Kisses

Makes 20

Cookie dough is a favorite and is made even more delicious with these little homemade chocolate kisses.

Prep: 25 mins, plus chilling   Cook: 12 mins, plus cooling

Ingredients

1 stick butter, softened

½ cup firmly packed light brown sugar

⅓ cup granulated sugar

½ teaspoon vanilla extract

1 egg

2 cups all-purpose flour

½ teaspoon baking soda

½ cup chocolate chips

8 ounces semisweet chocolate

¼ cup heavy cream

1. Preheat the oven to 350°F. Line three baking sheets with wax paper or silicone sheets. Whisk together the butter, brown sugar, and granulated sugar until just combined. Add the vanilla extract and egg and beat until combined.

2. Sift together the flour and baking soda into a separate bowl, then gradually add to the butter mixture until just combined. Fold through the chocolate chips and bring the dough together with your hands. Wrap in plastic wrap and chill in the refrigerator for 30 minutes.

3. Put the chocolate and cream into a heatproof bowl set over a saucepan of gently simmering water and heat until the chocolate is melted. Let cool for 15 minutes, until it is just beginning to thicken.

4. Spoon the chocolate into a pastry bag fitted with a ½-inch round tip and set aside for 15 minutes, or until thick enough to pipe out chocolate drops. Pipe twenty ¾ x ¾-inch mounds onto one of the prepared baking sheets. Chill in the refrigerator until hard.

5. Make 20 even balls of cookie dough and place on the remaining prepared baking sheets, spaced well apart to allow for spreading. Bake in the preheated oven for 10 minutes, until just golden and slightly undercooked.

6. Let the cookies cool on the sheets for 15 minutes, then press a chocolate kiss into the center of each. Let stand on the sheets to cool completely.

VARIATION

Want to eat the cookie dough raw? Omit the egg and add 1–2 tablespoons of milk. Chill the dough and eat it unbaked.

MILK & COOKIE
Shots

Refreshing almond milk served in a chocolate-lined, whole-grain hazelnut cookie—who said eating healthily was dull?

Prep: 35 mins, plus chilling   Cook: 18–20 mins

Ingredients

1 tablespoon coconut oil, for oiling

⅓ cup coconut oil, at room temperature

¼ cup firmly packed light brown sugar

½ teaspoon natural vanilla extract

¼ cup ground hazelnuts

¼ cup ground golden flaxseed

1 cup whole wheat-flour

1 egg yolk

4 ounces bittersweet chocolate

⅔ cup unsweetened almond milk

1. Lightly oil six 3oz rum baba molds and line each bottom with a disk of nonstick parchment paper.

2. Beat together the coconut oil, sugar, and vanilla extract in a mixing bowl or food processor until light and creamy. Add the hazelnuts and flaxseed, then add the flour and egg yolk and beat together. Finely chop 1 ounce of the chocolate and mix into the cookie crumbs. Using your hands, squeeze the dough into crumbly clumps.

3. Divide the dough among the prepared molds, then level with the back of a teaspoon. Transfer to a baking sheet and chill in the refrigerator for 20 minutes. Meanwhile, preheat the oven to 350°F.

4. Bake in the preheated oven for 13–15 minutes, until golden brown, then reshape the inside of the cups with the back of a small teaspoon. Let cool for 30 minutes.

5. Loosen the edges of the cups with a small, blunt knife and remove from the pan. Return to the baking sheet and chill in the refrigerator for at least 1 hour, until firmly set.

6. Break the remaining chocolate into a bowl set over a saucepan of gently simmering water and heat until melted. Add spoonfuls of melted chocolate to the cookie cups, tilting to cover the insides evenly with chocolate. Chill for at least 30 minutes. When ready to serve, pour in the almond milk and serve on small saucers.

NIBBLE

When choosing chocolate, it's useful to know what to look for in terms of quality.
Confusingly, chocolate classification and labeling requirements vary among
countries. The important factor is the ingredients list on the wrapper. Beware if
sugar appears near the top of the list—it means that it makes up a large proportion
of the chocolate and the quality will be inferior.

Eating chocolate

There are three basic types:

Dark: This is made from cocoa solids sweetened with sugar and blended with extra cocoa
butter. Top-quality dark chocolate contains a proportionately small amount of sugar. The higher
the proportion of cocoa solids, the better the chocolate. Bittersweet chocolate should have at
least 50 percent cocoa solids, but for chocoholics 70–80 percent is even better. Semisweet
chocolate has a higher proportion of sugar compared to cocoa solids.

Milk: This contains milk solids, cocoa butter, and sugar. A good brand will have about
40 percent cocoa solids, but most mass-produced milk chocolate contains only 20 percent
with a correspondingly high amount of sugar, sometimes up to 60 percent, to make up
the bulk.

White: This is a mixture of cocoa butter, milk solids, and up to 60 percent sugar. It usually
contains no cocoa solids and as such, lacks depth of flavor; it can seize when heated.
Sometimes synthetic vanilla is added to give it a boost.

How to recognize quality

When we try to assess chocolate quality, all our senses—sight, smell, sound, touch, and
taste—come into play:

Appearance: Dark chocolate should be smooth, shiny, and dark mahogany in color.

Smell: Chocolate should smell of chocolate and not excessively sweet.

Sound: Chocolate should be crisp and make a distinct "snap" when broken.

Touch: Chocolate with a high cocoa butter content should start to melt when you hold it. In
the mouth it should feel ultrasmooth and melt instantly.

Taste: Quality chocolate contains complex flavors and aromas. There should be bitterness
with a hint of acidity, sweetness tempered by a hint of sourness, and just a touch of saltiness
to help release the aromas.

Storing chocolate

Humidity and heat are chocolate's greatest enemies; both can cause a "bloom" to appear on
the surface. The ideal temperature is 50–59°F—slightly warmer than the refrigerator—and the
humidity level should be about 50 percent. Chocolate absorbs surrounding odors easily, even
when wrapped, so store it in an airtight container.

DARK CHOCOLATE &
Peanut Butter Energy Balls

Makes 8

These energizing healthy morsels, full of crunchy nuts, creamy peanut butter, and rich dark chocolate, have no added sugar.

Prep: 15 mins, plus chilling   Cook: None

Ingredients

½ cup ground almonds

¼ cup unsweetened peanut butter

2 tablespoons coarsely chopped unsalted peanuts

3 tablespoons flaxseed

1 ounce bittersweet chocolate, finely chopped

pinch of sea salt

1 teaspoon unsweetened cocoa powder

1. Put the ground almonds into a food processor and process for 1 minute, until you have the texture of coarse flour.

2. Put the peanut butter, peanuts, flaxseed, chocolate, and salt into a bowl and mix. Add the almond flour, reserving 1½ tablespoons. Mix until you have a texture resembling chunky clay.

3. Sprinkle the reserved almond flour and the cocoa powder onto a plate and mix with a teaspoon. Shape a tablespoon of the peanut mixture into a ball, using your palms. Roll it in the cocoa powder mixture, then transfer to a plate. Make another seven balls in the same way.

4. Cover and chill in the refrigerator for at least 30 minutes, or up to 2 days.

VARIATION

If the coating of cocoa powder is too bitter and strong for your taste, substitute it with a teaspoon of ground cinnamon.

INDULGENT WHISKEY
Fudge

Makes
16

If you are a chocolate- and whiskey-lover, this is the perfect edible treat for you. You can use a good brandy instead of whiskey, if you prefer.

Prep: 15 mins   Cook: 10–15 mins, plus setting

Ingredients

1 tablespoon sunflower oil, for oiling

1¼ cups firmly packed light brown sugar

1 stick unsalted butter, diced

1 (14-ounce) can sweetened condensed milk

2 tablespoons light corn syrup

6 ounces semisweet chocolate, coarsely chopped

¼ cup whiskey, preferrably Scotch whisky

¼ cup walnut pieces

1. Lightly brush an 8-inch square baking pan with the oil. Line it with nonstick parchment paper, snipping diagonally into the corners, then pressing the paper into the pan so that the bottom and sides are lined.

2. Put the sugar, butter, condensed milk, and corn syrup into a heavy saucepan. Heat gently, stirring constantly, until the sugar has dissolved.

3. Increase the heat and boil for 12–15 minutes, or until the mixture reaches 240°F on a candy thermometer (if you don't have a candy thermometer, spoon a little of the syrup into some iced water; it will form a soft ball when it is ready). As the temperature rises, stir the fudge occasionally so that the sugar doesn't stick and burn. Remove the fudge from the heat. Add the chocolate and whiskey and stir together until the chocolate has melted and the mixture is smooth.

4. Preheat the broiler to medium-hot. Put the walnuts in a baking pan and toast them under the broiler for 2–3 minutes, or until brown, then coarsely chop.

5. Pour the mixture into the prepared pan, smooth the surface with a spatula, and sprinkle with the walnuts. Let cool for 1 hour. Cover with plastic wrap, then chill in the refrigerator for 1–2 hours, or until firm. Lift the fudge out of the pan, peel off the paper, and cut into 16 squares. Store in an airtight container in a cool, dry place for up to 2 weeks.

CHOCOLATE TOFFEE
Popcorn

Serves 6–8

Planning a movie night in? Treat everyone with little individual bags of popcorn.

Prep: 10 mins, plus setting   Cook: 10–15 mins

Ingredients

3 tablespoons sunflower oil

¼ cup popping corn

3 tablespoons butter

¼ cup firmly packed
light brown sugar

2½ tablespoons light
corn syrup

2 ounces semisweet chocolate

⅔ cup crushed toffees

½ cup semisweet
chocolate chips

1. Lightly oil a large baking sheet and two wooden spoons with 1 tablespoon of the oil. Heat the rest of the oil in a large saucepan and add the popping corn. Cover with a lid and shake gently to coat with the oil.

2. Reduce the heat to low. Once you hear the corn popping, shake the pan occasionally and pay attention to the speed of the pops—when it has almost stopped, remove the pan from the heat.

3. Put the butter, sugar, and corn syrup into a separate, large saucepan and heat over medium heat until the sugar has dissolved. Increase the heat and boil gently for 2 minutes.

4. Add the popcorn to the pan of toffee and use the prepared spoons to toss until evenly coated. Transfer to the prepared baking sheet and let set.

5. Meanwhile, put the chocolate into a heatproof bowl set over a saucepan of gently simmering water and heat until melted.

6. Sprinkle the popcorn with the crushed toffees and chocolate chips and drizzle with the melted chocolate. Let set before serving. Store in a sealed container in a cool, dry place.

VARIATION
Want to speed things up? Use 6 cups popcorn instead of popping your own.

PEPPERMINT
Creams

Makes 25

The pretty and tasty peppermint cream is an old-fashioned favorite. It's a refreshing choice for an after-dinner treat.

Prep: 30 mins, plus setting   Cook: 5 mins

Ingredients

1 extra-large egg white

2⅔ cups confectioners' sugar, sifted

2–4 drops peppermint extract

2–4 drops green food coloring

1 tablespoon confectioners' sugar, for dipping

4 ounces semisweet chocolate, coarsely chopped

1. Line a baking sheet with nonstick parchment paper.

2. Lightly whisk the egg white in a large, clean mixing bowl until it is frothy but still translucent.

3. Add the sifted confectioners' sugar to the egg white and stir with a wooden spoon until the mixture is stiff. Knead in the peppermint extract and food coloring.

4. Using the palms of your hands, roll the mixture into walnut-size balls and place them on the prepared baking sheet. Use a fork to flatten them; if it sticks to them, dip it in confectioners' sugar before pressing. Put the creams into the refrigerator to set for 24 hours.

5. Put the chocolate in a heatproof bowl set over a saucepan of gently simmering water and heat until melted. Dip the creams halfway into the chocolate vertically and return to the baking sheet for 1 hour, or until set. Store in an airtight container in the refrigerator for up to 5 days.

CHOCOLATE & HAZELNUT
Cake pops

Makes 20

Creamy chocolate-hazelnut spread and delicious chopped, toasted hazelnuts add a smooth flavor and crunchy texture to these addictive little bites.

Prep: 30 mins, plus chilling   Cook: 30 mins, plus setting

Ingredients

2 eggs

¼ cup firmly packed light brown sugar

¼ cup superfine or granulated sugar

¾ cup all-purpose flour, sifted

1 stick butter, melted

1 teaspoon baking powder

2 tablespoons unsweetened cocoa powder, sifted

1 teaspoon vanilla extract

2 cups chocolate-hazelnut spread

Decoration

12 ounces semisweet chocolate, broken into pieces

¾ cup skinned whole hazelnuts

20 lollipop sticks or wooden toothpicks

1. Preheat the oven to 400°F. Line an 7-inch round cake pan and a baking sheet with parchment paper.

2. Put the eggs, brown sugar, and superfine sugar into a bowl and beat well until light and frothy.

3. Lightly fold in the flour, butter, baking powder, cocoa powder, and vanilla extract. Let stand for 20 minutes. Pour into the prepared cake pan and bake in the preheated oven for 15–20 minutes, or until a toothpick inserted in the middle of the cake comes out clean. Let cool in the pan for 10 minutes, then transfer to a wire rack to cool completely.

4. Use your fingertips to crumble the cooled cake into a mixing bowl. Stir in the chocolate-hazelnut spread and mix together with a fork. Use an ice-cream scoop to remove a golf-ball-size piece of the mixture, then use your hands to shape it into a ball. Place on the prepared baking sheet. Repeat with the remaining mixture to make 20 balls, then transfer to the refrigerator to chill for at least 30 minutes.

5. To make the decoration, put the chocolate into a heatproof bowl set over a saucepan of gently simmering water and heat until melted.

6. Place the hazelnuts in a dry skillet and heat for 2–3 minutes, stirring constantly to prevent them from burning. Transfer the toasted nuts to a cutting board and coarsely chop.

7. When ready to decorate the cake balls, insert a lollipop stick into each one and dip the cakes in the melted chocolate, using a teaspoon to help you to coat them completely. Return to the baking sheet and sprinkle the top of each cake with hazelnuts. Transfer to a glass and let set.

CHOCOLATE & CARAMEL
Cups

Makes 12

If you don't have any petit four cases, line the cups in a mini muffin pan with small squares of plastic wrap and spread the melted chocolate over them—don't forget to peel away the plastic before serving.

Prep: 30 mins   Cook: 7–8 mins, plus chilling

Ingredients

6 ounces semisweet chocolate, coarsely chopped

½ cup granulated sugar

¼ cup water

12 small walnut halves

2 tablespoons unsalted butter

½ cup heavy cream

1. Line a 12-cup mini muffin pan with a double layer of paper petit four liners. Line a baking sheet with nonstick parchment paper.

2. Put the chocolate into a heatproof bowl, set the bowl over a saucepan of gently simmering water, and heat until melted. Put a spoonful of melted chocolate into each paper liner, then evenly brush over the sides using a small pastry brush. Chill in the refrigerator for 30 minutes, then brush on a second layer of chocolate, taking care with the sides so that there is an even thickness. Cover and chill in the refrigerator.

3. Put the sugar and water into a small, heavy saucepan. Heat gently for 5 minutes, or until the sugar has dissolved, tilting the pan to mix them together. Increase the heat and boil rapidly without stirring for 4–5 minutes, until the caramel is deep golden, being careful that it doesn't burn. Remove from the heat, add the walnuts, quickly coat them in the caramel, then lift them out, using two forks. Put them on the prepared baking sheet, spaced slightly apart.

4. Add the butter to the remaining caramel, tilt the pan to mix, then gradually stir in the cream. Transfer to a bowl, let cool, then cover and chill in the refrigerator for 1½ hours, or until thick. Lift the chocolate-lined paper liners out of the pan. Spoon the caramel cream into a large pastry bag fitted with a large star tip and pipe it into the chocolate cups. Chill in the refrigerator until required. Decorate the cups with the caramel walnuts just before serving.

CHOCOLATE "SALAMI" Log

It's nice to have a little treat on hand when you have friends over. You'll be sneaking back to the refrigerator for just a little more of this "salami."

Serves 12

Prep: 10 mins, plus chilling   Cook: 8 mins

Ingredients

¾ cup blanched hazelnuts

⅓ cup slivered almonds

½ cup coarsely chopped dried figs

2 tablespoons triple sec

7 ounces semisweet chocolate

6 tablespoons butter

½ cup firmly packed light brown sugar

1 extra-large egg, plus 1 extra-large egg yolk

zest of 1 orange

1 (7-ounce) package amaretti cookies

¼ cup white chocolate chips

1 tablespoon confectioners' sugar, for dusting

1. Put the hazelnuts and almonds into a large, heavy skillet and heat over high heat, stirring frequently, until golden brown. Let cool slightly, then coarsely chop.

2. Put the figs and triple sec into a microwave-proof bowl and heat on High for 1 minute. Set aside.

3. Put the chocolate and butter into a heatproof bowl set over a saucepan of gently simmering water and heat until melted.

4. Meanwhile, beat together the sugar, egg, egg yolk, and orange zest in a separate bowl until thick and combined. Transfer to the chocolate mixture and stir for 5 minutes, or until the sugar is completely dissolved.

5. Crush the cookies into smallish chunks and fold through the chocolate mixture with the figs, nuts, and chocolate chips until evenly coated. Spoon the mixture onto a piece of wax paper, shaping into an 8-inch log. Tightly roll up the log, twisting both ends to secure. Chill in the refrigerator for 4 hours or overnight.

6. Remove from the refrigerator, dust with the confectioners' sugar, and serve. Store in the refrigerator.

VARIATION
Use your favorite
dried fruit and soak in
your preferred liquor—
rum, brandy, or
amaretto.

DOUBLE CHOCOLATE
Pecan Blondies

Makes 12

With chunks of white and dark chocolate and crunchy pecans, these addictive bars are an indulgent treat.

Prep: 30 mins, plus cooling   Cook: 35–40 mins

Ingredients

9 ounces white chocolate, broken into pieces

3 tablespoons butter, plus extra for greasing

6 ounces semisweet chocolate

2 extra-large eggs, beaten

⅓ cup superfine or granulated sugar

1 cup all-purpose flour

1 teaspoon baking powder

1 cup coarsely chopped pecans

1. Preheat the oven to 350°F. Grease an 8-inch square shallow baking pan or baking dish.

2. Put 3 ounces of the white chocolate and all the butter into a heatproof bowl set over a saucepan of gently simmering water and heat, stirring occasionally, until melted and smooth. Meanwhile, coarsely chop the remaining white chocolate and semisweet chocolate.

3. Beat together the eggs and sugar in a large bowl, then stir in the melted chocolate mixture. Sift the flour and baking powder over the top. Add the chopped chocolate and pecans. Mix well.

4. Spoon the mixture into the prepared pan and smooth the surface. Bake in the preheated oven for 35–40 minutes, or until golden brown and just firm to the touch in the center. Let stand in the pan to cool completely, then turn out and cut into 12 bars.

TIP
Be careful to avoid overcooking the blondies or you'll lose the lovely soft, squishy texture.

DARK CHOCOLATE &
Amaretto Truffles

Makes 12

These delectable morsels are so easy to make and look really glamorous.
Use any liqueur instead of the amaretto, if you prefer.

Prep: 30 mins, plus soaking and setting   Cook: 5–10 mins

Ingredients

¼ cup amaretto liqueur

⅓ cup golden raisins

4 ounces semisweet chocolate, coarsely chopped

2 tablespoons heavy cream

⅛ chocolate cake (about 8 inches in diameter), crumbled

1 cup hazelnuts

¼ cup chocolate sprinkles, to decorate

1. Put the amaretto and golden raisins into a small mixing bowl, cover, and let soak for 6–8 hours. Line a baking sheet with nonstick parchment paper.

2. Transfer the amaretto mixture to a food processor and process until pureed.

3. Put the chocolate and cream into a heatproof bowl set over a saucepan of gently simmering water and heat until the chocolate is melted. Remove from the heat, add the amaretto puree and chocolate cake, and stir well.

4. When cool enough to handle, use the palms of your hands to roll the mixture into truffle-size balls. Place them on the prepared baking sheet.

5. Preheat the broiler to medium. Put the hazelnuts on a baking sheet and toast them under the broiler for 2–3 minutes, or until brown, shaking them halfway through. Finely chop them.

6. Spread the chocolate sprinkles on one plate and sprinkle the hazelnuts on another. Roll half the truffles in the chocolate sprinkles and half in the hazelnuts.

7. Return to the baking sheet, cover with nonstick parchment paper, and chill in the refrigerator for 1–2 hours, or until firm. Store in an airtight container in the refrigerator for up to 5 days.

SOFT

HOT CHOCOLATE
Layer Cake

Serves 8

With a super-speedy cake batter, a store-bought chocolate frosting, and some whipped cream, you really can create a rich and indulgent chocolate cake in 30 minutes.

Prep: 30 mins, plus cooling   Cook: 12–15 mins

Ingredients

½ tablespoon butter, for greasing

3 eggs

⅓ cup superfine or granulated sugar

⅔ cup all-purpose flour

2 tablespoons unsweetened cocoa powder

1 tablespoon sugar, for dusting

1 cup heavy cream

1 cup ready-to-eat chocolate frosting

dark and white chocolate shavings or curls, to decorate (optional)

2 tablespoons unsweetened cocoa powder, for dusting

1. Preheat the oven to 400°F. Lightly grease a 9 x 13-inch rectangular baking pan and line the bottom and sides with parchment paper.

2. Put the eggs and sugar into a large bowl set over a saucepan of gently simmering water. Beat with a handheld electric mixer for 3–4 minutes, or until the mixture is thick and pale.

3. Sift in the flour and cocoa powder and gently fold in. Pour into the prepared pan and level the surface. Bake in the preheated oven for 8–10 minutes, or until risen and springy to the touch. Meanwhile, dust a sheet of parchment paper with superfine sugar and whip the cream until it holds firm peaks.

4. Remove the cake from the oven and immediately turn out onto the prepared parchment paper. Cut the cake into three strips and transfer to a wire rack to cool for 5–8 minutes.

5. Spread the frosting over the top of each strip and sandwich the strips together with the cream. Decorate with the chocolate shavings or curls, if using, and dust with the cocoa powder.

TIP
The beaten batter should be thick enough to leave a ribbon-like trail on the surface when the beaters are lifted.

CHILE & CHOCOLATE
Churros

Makes 16

Chile and chocolate are frequently used together in South American cooking and make a surprisingly good flavor combination.

Prep: 20 mins, plus cooling   Cook: 25 mins

Ingredients

1 stick unsalted butter, diced

1 cup water

1¼ cups all-purpose flour, sifted

large pinch of salt

2 extra-large eggs, beaten

½ small red chile, seeded and finely chopped

oil, for deep-frying

¼ cup sugar

2 teaspoons unsweetened cocoa powder, sifted

Chocolate Sauce

3 ounces semisweet chocolate, broken into pieces

½ cup heavy cream

½ teaspoon vanilla extract

1 teaspoon crushed red pepper flakes

1. To make the chocolate sauce, put the chocolate and cream into a heatproof bowl set over a saucepan of gently simmering water and heat until the chocolate is melted. Remove from the heat and stir until smooth, then stir in the vanilla extract and red pepper flakes. Set aside and keep warm.

2. Put the butter and water into a large saucepan over low heat and heat until the butter has melted. Bring to a boil, remove from the heat, and add the flour and salt. Beat thoroughly until the mixture is smooth and comes away from the side of the pan. Let cool for 5 minutes, then gradually beat in the eggs to make a thick and glossy paste. Beat in the chile.

3. Heat enough oil for deep-frying in a large saucepan or deep fryer to 350–375°F, or until a cube of bread browns in 30 seconds. Spoon the paste into a large pastry bag fitted with a large star tip and pipe four 4-inch lengths of the paste into the hot oil. Fry for 2–3 minutes, turning frequently, until crisp and golden. Remove with a slotted spoon and drain on paper towels. Keep warm while frying the remaining mixture.

4. Mix together the sugar and cocoa powder on a flat plate and toss the warm churros in the mixture, in batches, to coat. Serve immediately with the chocolate sauce for dipping.

TIP
Dark chocolate has more cacao and less sugar than other chocolate, so it is healthier than milk and white chocolates.

MOLTEN MARSHMALLOW
Chocolate Chunk Brownies

Makes 12

Prep: 20 mins, plus cooling   Cook: 25 mins

Brownies just got even better—chocolate and marshmallow are perfectly paired in this wonderfully gooey mess.

Ingredients

2¼ sticks unsalted butter, plus ½ tablespoon for greasing

9 ounces semisweet chocolate

4 extra-extra-large eggs

1¾ cups superfine or granulated sugar

1½ teaspoons vanilla extract

½ teaspoon salt

1¼ cups all-purpose flour

3 ounces large chocolate disks or chocolate chunks

¾ cup marshmallow creme

1. Preheat the oven to 350°F. Grease an 8½-inch square baking pan and line with parchment paper.

2. Put the butter and chocolate into a heatproof bowl set over a saucepan of gently simmering water and heat, stirring occasionally, until melted. Remove from the heat and let cool slightly. Beat together the eggs, sugar, vanilla extract, and salt in a bowl.

3. Beat the egg mixture into the cooled chocolate mixture, then fold in the flour. Stir in half the chocolate disks, pour into the prepared pan, and bake in the preheated oven for 30 minutes.

4. Carefully remove the brownie from the oven (do not turn off the oven). Add spoonfuls of the marshmallow creme to the top.

5. Sprinkle with the remaining chocolate disks and bake for an additional 10–15 minutes, until the marshmallow is molten and beginning to brown. Let cool slightly, then cut into 12 squares and serve.

Soft

CHOCOLATE & SAFFRON
Brioches

Makes 12

Saffron will add a subtle and sophisticated flavor to your baking. It's also said to have aphrodisiac qualities, so these brioches would be perfect for a Valentine's Day brunch.

Prep: 35 mins, plus proving and cooling   Cook: 45 mins

Ingredients

pinch of saffron threads

3 tablespoons boiling water

½ tablespoon butter, melted, for greasing

4 tablespoons butter, melted

2¾ cups all-purpose flour

pinch of salt

1 tablespoon superfine or granulated sugar

2½ teaspoons active dry yeast

2 eggs, beaten

6 small squares semisweet chocolate, halved

1 tablespoon milk, for glazing

1. Add the saffron to the boiling water and let cool completely.

2. Lightly brush 12 individual brioche pans or large fluted muffin cups with melted butter.

3. Sift together the flour, salt, and sugar into a bowl and stir in the yeast. Add the saffron liquid, eggs, and butter and stir to make a soft dough.

4. Knead until smooth, then cover and let stand in a warm place for 1–1½ hours, until doubled in size. Knead briefly, then shape three-quarters of the dough into 12 balls. Place one in every pan and press a piece of chocolate firmly into each.

5. Shape the remaining dough into small balls with a pointed end. Brush with milk and press the balls into each brioche, sealing well.

6. Cover with oiled plastic wrap and let stand in a warm place for 1½ hours, or until doubled in size. Meanwhile, preheat the oven to 400°F. Brush the brioches with the milk and bake in the preheated oven for 12–15 minutes, until firm and golden. Turn out and serve warm.

TIP

If you don't have a
mortar and pestle, put the
peppercorns into a plastic
bag and crush them with
a rolling pin.

PINK PEPPERCORN &
Chocolate Cupcakes

Makes 12

Pepper with chocolate is a surprising combination, but it works! Here, the crushed pink peppercorns provide a wonderful contrasting color as well as flavor.

Prep: 35 mins, plus cooling   Cook: 25 mins

Ingredients

1 cup all-purpose flour

¾ cup unsweetened cocoa powder

1 teaspoon baking powder

¼ teaspoon salt

1 stick unsalted butter, softened

1 cup superfine or granulated sugar

2 teaspoons vanilla extract

2 extra-large eggs

½ cup sour cream

1 tablespoon pink peppercorns, crushed, to decorate

Frosting

¼ cup milk

1 tablespoon pink peppercorns, crushed

1 stick unsalted butter, softened

2 cups confectioners' sugar

2 teaspoons vanilla extract

1. Preheat the oven to 350°F and line a 12-cup cupcake pan with paper liners.

2. Sift together the flour, cocoa powder, baking powder, and salt into a bowl. Put the butter and superfine sugar into a separate bowl and beat until pale and fluffy. Add the vanilla extract, then add the eggs, one at a time, beating after each addition. Add half of the flour mixture and the sour cream and beat until combined. Add the remaining flour mixture and mix.

3. Spoon the batter into the paper liners and bake in the preheated oven for 20 minutes, until risen and a toothpick inserted into the center of a cupcake comes out clean. Let cool in the pan for 1–2 minutes, then transfer to a wire rack to cool completely.

4. Meanwhile, to make the frosting, put the milk and peppercorns into a small saucepan and heat over medium heat until just boiling. Reduce the heat to low and simmer for about 5 minutes, stirring frequently. Strain the milk into a bowl, discarding the peppercorns, and let cool for about 10 minutes.

5. Add the butter, confectioners' sugar, and vanilla extract to the milk and beat with a handheld electric mixer until well combined. Add more confectioners' sugar, if necessary, to achieve a pastry consistency. Spoon the frosting into a pastry bag fitted with a star-shape tip and pipe onto the cupcakes.

6. To decorate, sprinkle a little of the crushed pink peppercorns over the tops of the cupcakes.

MINI CHOCOLATE
Whoopie Pies

Who would have thought you could make these treats in such a short time? For a special treat, replace the chocolate spread with whipped cream and preserves.

Makes 22

Prep: 20 mins, plus cooling and chilling   Cook: 8 mins

Ingredients

1 cup butter, softened

½ cup firmly packed dark brown sugar

1 egg, lightly beaten

½ teaspoon vanilla extract

1⅓ cups all-purpose flour

1¼ cup baking powder

¼ cup unsweetened cocoa powder

⅓ cup milk

¼–⅓ cup chocolate-hazelnut spread

1. Preheat the oven to 375°F. Line two large baking sheets with parchment paper.

2. Put the butter and sugar into a large bowl and beat with a handheld electric mixer for 1–2 minutes. Whisk in the egg and vanilla extract. Sift in the flour, baking powder, and cocoa powder, add the milk, and gently fold in until thoroughly combined.

3. Pipe or spoon 44 small mounds of the batter onto the prepared baking sheet. Each mound should be about 1½ inches in diameter. Bake in the preheated oven for 7–8 minutes, or until just firm. Carefully transfer the hot cakes to a wire rack, using a spatula. Let cool for 10 minutes.

4. Sandwich the cakes together with the chocolate-hazelnut spread. If the spread starts to soften because the cakes are still slightly warm, put the filled whoopie pies in the refrigerator for a few minutes, until completely cold.

TIP
To speed up the cooling process, gently flip the cakes over on the rack after 5 minutes.

White Chocolate & Blackberry Muffins

Makes 12

Muffins are so simple to make. You can whip up a batch tonight and slip one into everyone's lunch box for a treat tomorrow.

Prep: 10–15 mins   Cook: 25–30 mins

Ingredients

2⅓ cups all-purpose flour

1 teaspoon baking powder

1 cup superfine or granulated sugar

1 stick unsalted butter

2 eggs

1 tablespoon vanilla extract

1 cup low-fat plain yogurt

1⅓ cups blackberries

7 ounces white chocolate, chopped into chunks

1. Preheat the oven to 350°F. Line a 12-cup muffin pan with paper liners.

2. Sift together the flour, baking powder, and sugar into a large bowl. In a separate bowl, beat together the butter, eggs, vanilla extract, and yogurt until combined.

3. Fold the egg mixture into the flour mixture until just combined. Stir in the blackberries and chocolate.

4. Spoon the batter evenly into the paper liners and bake in the preheated oven for 25–30 minutes, until golden and cooked through. The muffins should bounce back when pressed gently with a finger. Transfer to a wire rack to cool.

TIP

The secret of a good muffin is not to overmix. It's fine if some flour is still showing when you put them in the oven.

CHUNKY CHOCOLATE
Bread & Butter Pudding

Serves 6–8

Lift bread and butter pudding into the realms of luxury with the addition of dark chocolate and sweet dried figs. Serve with a little cream for a real treat.

Prep: 10 mins, plus cooling   Cook: 35–40 mins

Ingredients

1 large brioche loaf
1¾ sticks butter, softened
6 ounces bittersweet chocolate, broken into large pieces
½ cup chopped dried figs
4 extra-large eggs
2½ cups milk
¾ cup superfine or granulated sugar
1 teaspoon vanilla extract

1. Preheat the oven to 325°F.

2. Line a 9 x 5 x 3-inch loaf pan with parchment paper.

3. Slice the brioche and butter each slice on one side. Sprinkle the chocolate and figs over the buttered side of the slices. Put the slices back into the shape of the loaf and fit it into the prepared pan.

4. In a medium bowl, whisk together the eggs, milk, sugar, and vanilla extract, then pour the mixture over the brioche and let soak for 5 minutes.

5. Bake in the preheated oven for 35–40 minutes, or until golden and the liquid has set in the middle. Remove from the oven and let cool for 10 minutes before serving.

SOFT

When you bake or decorate with chocolate, the better the raw materials, the better the result.

Chocolate for cooking

Good-quality dark chocolate has an intense flavor and rich, dark color that are ideal for desserts and cakes. Milk and white chocolate are less intense in flavor but are useful for creating contrasting color.

Couverture chocolate

The king of cooking chocolate, this has a high cocoa butter content, so it melts smoothly and forms a thin, crisp coating when tempered and cooled. Couverture chocolate is used mainly for molding and coating handmade chocolates.

Disks and chips

These keep their shape when baked, and they also melt easily and evenly into batters and doughs, so you don't need to chop up a chocolate bar into uneven chunks. They contain less cocoa butter than bars, but they're ideal for using in cakes and chocolate chip cookies.

Chocolate-candy coating disks

Easier to melt and handle than dark chocolate, these work well for decorations and for coating cakes. The disadvantage is that some or all of the cocoa butter has been replaced by other fats, such as coconut oil or palm oil, so the taste and texture aren't as refined as those of chocolate bars.

Cocoa powder

Not to be confused with sweetened hot cocoa mix, cocoa powder is probably the most economical way of giving cakes and desserts a good chocolate flavor.

How to melt

When you use chocolate in cakes and desserts, it usually needs melting. Like mayonnaise, chocolate is basically an emulsion of different liquids that will separate if mistreated. If you melt it at too high a heat, it will "seize" (split), turn grainy, or even burn. Along with heat, water is an enemy, too. A single drop or even a puff of steam will cause seizing, so make sure your saucepan and utensils are absolutely dry.

In the microwave

Dark chocolate: Microwave on Medium for about 2 minutes.
Milk and white chocolate: Microwave on Low for about 2 minutes.
The chocolate will not change shape but will start to look shiny. Check and stir every 30 seconds.

In a low oven

Preheat the oven to 225°F. Chop the chocolate, put it into an ovenproof bowl, and heat in the oven for a few minutes. Remove before completely melted and stir until smooth.

Over simmering water

Chop the chocolate into small pieces so that it melts quickly and evenly. Put it into a dry, heatproof bowl set over a saucepan of gently simmering water, making sure the bottom of the bowl isn't touching the water. The bowl should fit really snugly over the saucepan so that steam can't escape and make the chocolate seize. Heat gently, stirring occasionally, until smooth.

Over direct heat

This can be done only if the recipe includes a heated liquid, such as milk or cream. The heat of the liquid protects the chocolate and helps to melt it. Gently heat the liquid in a heavy saucepan over low heat. Stir in the chopped chocolate, then stir until smooth. Immediately remove from the heat.

White Chocolate &
Passion Fruit Éclairs

Makes 10

These light, fruity éclairs look delicious with a white chocolate topping and have a distinctly tropical flavor—perfect for summer occasions.

Prep: 30 mins, plus cooling and standing   Cook: 45 mins

Ingredients

4 tablespoons butter

⅔ cup water

½ cup all-purpose flour, sifted

pinch of salt

2 extra-large eggs, beaten

1 cup heavy cream

2 passion fruit

Topping

8 ounces white chocolate, broken into pieces

yellow writing icing (optional)

1. Preheat the oven to 400°F. Line two baking sheets with parchment paper.

2. Put the butter and water into a medium saucepan and bring to a boil. Add the flour and salt and beat well until the mixture starts to come away from the side of the pan. Remove from the heat and let cool for 1–2 minutes.

3. Gradually beat in the eggs until the mixture is smooth and glossy. Transfer to a pastry bag fitted with a 1-inch tip and pipe ten 3¼-inch lengths of the batter onto the prepared baking sheets.

4. Bake in the preheated oven for 15 minutes, then remove from the oven and make a fine slit along the length of each éclair to let the steam escape. Return to the oven and bake for an additional 10 minutes, then transfer to a wire rack to cool.

5. Whip the cream until it just holds stiff peaks. Cut the passion fruit in half and use a teaspoon to remove the flesh. Stir into the cream and use either a pastry bag or a teaspoon to fill the éclairs with the mixture.

6. To make the topping, put the chocolate into a heatproof bowl set over a saucepan of gently simmering water and heat until melted. Use a teaspoon to spread the melted chocolate evenly over the filled éclairs. To create a feathered effect, pipe 2–3 straight lines lengthwise on the chocolate with the writing icing, if using. Carefully drag a toothpick back and forth across the lines at regular intervals. Let stand for 30 minutes before serving.

CHOCOLATE CAKE
Donuts

Makes 14

These delicious donuts are made without yeast, so they're much quicker to prepare than normal donuts and you'll get them to the table faster.

Prep: 25 mins, plus resting   Cook: 55 mins

Ingredients

½ cup lukewarm milk

1 egg

1 teaspoon vanilla extract

⅓ cup unsweetened cocoa powder

1⅓ cups all-purpose flour

½ teaspoon baking soda

½ teaspoon baking powder

½ teaspoon salt

½ cup superfine or granulated sugar

2 tablespoons butter, melted

1 tablespoon flour, for dusting

oil, for deep-frying

Glaze

2 ounces semisweet chocolate, broken into pieces

2 ounces white chocolate, broken into pieces

1. Blend together the milk, egg, and vanilla extract in a bowl.

2. Using a stand mixer with a flat beater, mix together the cocoa powder, flour, baking soda, baking powder, salt, and sugar. Add the butter and blend. Slowly add the milk, egg, and vanilla mixture. Mix until the batter is smooth and thick and resembles a cookie dough.

3. Let the dough rest in the mixer for 20 minutes.

4. Turn out the dough on a floured work surface and roll out to a thickness of ½ inch. Use a donut cutter to stamp out 14 donuts.

5. Heat enough oil for deep-frying in a large saucepan or deep fryer to 350–375°F, or until a cube of bread browns in 30 seconds. Carefully place the donuts, one at a time, into the oil. Cook for 2 minutes on each side, or until golden brown. Remove with a slotted spoon and drain on paper towels.

6. To make the glaze, put the semisweet chocolate and white chocolate into separate heatproof bowls set over saucepans of gently simmering water and heat until melted. Use the semisweet chocolate to coat 7 donuts and the white chocolate to coat the remaining donuts, drizzling a contrasting pattern over the coating when set.

VARIATION
You could replace the semisweet and white chocolate with milk chocolate, if you prefer.

TIP
When adding the egg
whites to the melted
chocolate, beat them
in quickly so that the
chocolate doesn't
seize.

CHOCOLATE MOUSSE
Brownie Layered Desserts

Show off these little layered puddings by serving them in straight glasses.
They will look spectacular and are bound to impress.

Makes 4

Prep: 30 mins, plus chilling   Cook: 5 mins

Ingredients

4 ounces white chocolate,
finely chopped

4 extra-large egg whites

2 tablespoons superfine or
granulated sugar

4 brownie squares

½ cup dulce de leche
(caramel sauce)

½ cup heavy cream

1 teaspoon unsweetened
cocoa powder, to decorate

1. Put the chocolate into a heatproof bowl set over a saucepan of gently simmering water and heat until melted.

2. Whisk the egg whites in a grease-free bowl until they hold soft peaks. Add the sugar and whisk until they hold firm peaks.

3. Spoon one-third of the egg whites into the melted chocolate and beat in. Using a large metal spoon, gently fold in the remaining egg whites until well combined.

4. Trim the brownies into circles that will fit snugly in the glasses, reserving the scraps. Slice the brownies in half horizontally.

5. Divide half the chocolate mousse mixture among four small jars or glasses with straight sides. Carefully top each with a slice of brownie, then drizzle with 1 tablespoon of the dulce de leche. Work carefully, defining the layers. Repeat the layers one time.

6. Lightly whip the cream and spoon it over the layered desserts. Crumble the reserved brownie scraps over the top and sprinkle with a pinch of cocoa powder. Transfer to the refrigerator for 4 hours or overnight to chill and set.

Cocoa & Cinnamon
Madeleines with White Chocolate

Makes 12

These distinctive shell-shaped cakes are quintessentially French, and although dipping them into chocolate may not be traditional, they are definitely delicious.

Prep: 30 mins, plus standing and cooling   Cook: 15 mins

Ingredients

½ tablespoon melted butter, for greasing

1 tablespoon flour, for dusting

2 eggs

¼ cup firmly packed light brown sugar

¼ cup superfine or granulated sugar

¾ cup all-purpose flour, sifted

1 stick butter, melted

1 teaspoon baking powder

½ teaspoon ground cinnamon

2 tablespoons unsweetened cocoa powder, sifted

1 teaspoon vanilla extract

4 ounces white chocolate, broken into pieces, to decorate

1. Preheat the oven to 400°F. Lightly grease a 12-section madeleine pan and dust with flour.

2. Put the eggs, brown sugar, and superfine sugar into a mixing bowl and beat well until the mixture is light and frothy.

3. Lightly fold in the flour, butter, baking powder, cinnamon, cocoa powder, and vanilla extract. Let stand for 20 minutes.

4. Divide the batter among the sections in the prepared pan and bake in the preheated oven for 8–10 minutes, until well risen. Let cool in the pan for 1–2 minutes, then transfer to a wire rack to cool completely.

5. To decorate, put the chocolate into a heatproof bowl set over a saucepan of gently simmering water and heat until melted. Dip the end of each madeleine into the melted chocolate and let set on a baking sheet. Eat on the day of making.

PAIN-AU-CHOCOLAT
Cinnamon Rolls

Makes 12

Can't decide between a sweet cinnamon roll or a crisp and flaky pain au chocolat? Well, now you can enjoy the best of both with this delicious quick-and-easy hybrid of the two.

Prep: 20 mins, plus standing, chilling and cooling   Cook: 15–20 mins

Ingredients

4 ounces semisweet chocolate, broken into pieces

1 sheet ready-to-bake puff pastry, thawed if frozen

2 tablespoons unsalted butter, melted

2 tablespoons superfine or granulated sugar

1½ teaspoons ground cinnamon

1 tablespoon confectioners' sugar, for dusting

1. Put the chocolate into a heatproof bowl set over a saucepan of gently simmering water and heat until melted. Remove from the heat, stir until smooth, then let cool for 15 minutes, stirring occasionally.

2. Unroll the sheet of puff pastry and place on a board. Generously brush with some of the melted butter. Let stand for 10 minutes, then spread the cooled chocolate all over the buttered pastry. Mix together the sugar and cinnamon in a bowl, then sprinkle over the chocolate.

3. Roll up the pastry, jellyroll style, from one long side, then brush all over with more of the melted butter. Chill in the refrigerator for 15 minutes. Preheat the oven to 425°F. Use the remaining melted butter to grease a 12-cup cupcake pan.

4. Using a serrated knife, slice the pastry roll into 12 even circles. Put each circle into a cup in the prepared cupcake pan.

5. Bake in the preheated oven for 15–20 minutes, or until risen and golden brown. Let cool in the pan for 5 minutes, then transfer to a wire rack. Dust the rolls with confectioners' sugar and serve warm or cold.

VARIATION
For a mocha-flavored filling, replace the cinnamon with 2 teaspoons of instant coffee powder.

WHITE CHOCOLATE
Blondies

Makes 12

For a morning coffee treat, these soft, squishy blondies are hard to beat. Mixed in one bowl and baked in under 25 minutes, they are the perfect speedy baked good.

Prep: 15 mins, plus cooling   Cook: 22 mins

Ingredients

½ tablespoon butter, for greasing

1 stick butter

1 cup firmly packed light brown sugar

2 eggs

1 teaspoon vanilla extract

1¼ cups all-purpose flour

pinch of salt

½ cup white chocolate chips

1. Preheat the oven to 400°F. Lightly grease an 8-inch square shallow cake pan and line with parchment paper.

2. Put the butter into a small saucepan and melt over low heat. Transfer to a large bowl with the sugar, then beat with a wire whisk until combined.

3. Beat in the eggs and vanilla extract, then sift in the flour and salt and beat well until smooth. Pour the batter into the prepared pan and level the surface with a spatula. Sprinkle with the chocolate chips.

4. Bake in the preheated oven for 20–22 minutes, or until golden brown and just set (the center will still be a little soft). Let cool in the pan, then turn out and cut into 12 squares.

TIP
To save time, use a microwave-proof mixing bowl and melt the butter for 20-30 seconds on High.

CHOCOLATE-SWIRLED
Pumpkin Pie Slice

Serves 16

Pumpkin pie is an all-time favorite, but it has been made even better by adding a luxurious swirl of dark chocolate.

Prep: 25 mins, plus chilling   Cook: 1 hour

TIP
Keep an eye on the pie as it nears the end of the cooking time. If it's browning too quickly loosely cover with aluminum foil to retain the color of the pumpkin against the chocolate.

Ingredients

½ tablespoon butter, for greasing

28 graham crackers or plain cookies (about 7 ounces)

8 ounces semisweet chocolate

4 tablespoons unsalted butter, melted

1¾ cups cream cheese

2 cups superfine or granulated sugar

1¾ cups canned solid pumpkin puree

3 extra-large eggs

1 teaspoon vanilla extract

⅓ cup all-purpose flour

1 teaspoon ground cinnamon

½ teaspoon salt

1. Preheat the oven to 350°F. Grease a 10-inch square baking pan and line with parchment paper. Put the cookies into a food processor bowl and pulse to coarse crumbs.

2. Put 3 ounces of the chocolate into a heatproof bowl set over a saucepan of gently simmering water and heat until melted. Add the butter and the melted chocolate to the cookie crumbs and pulse to combine. Transfer to the prepared pan and press in firmly with the back of a spoon. Bake in the preheated oven for 12–15 minutes, then remove from the oven and let cool (do not turn off the oven).

3. Put the cream cheese into a bowl and lightly whisk until smooth. Add the sugar, pumpkin puree, eggs, vanilla extract, flour, cinnamon, and salt. Lightly whisk until the mixture is smooth and combined.

4. Put the remaining chocolate into a heatproof bowl set over a saucepan of gently simmering water and heat until melted. Remove from the heat and add about ¾ cup of the pumpkin mixture, stirring well to combine.

5. Pour the remaining pumpkin mixture into the prepared pan. Place large spoonfuls of the chocolate pumpkin mixture on the pumpkin mixture, then drag a knife through to create swirls.

6. Transfer to the oven and bake for 40–45 minutes. The pie should still have a slight wobble in the center. Let cool to room temperature, then wrap in plastic wrap and chill in the refrigerator for 2 hours or overnight until firm. Cut into 16 slices and serve.

ZEBRA CAKES WITH
Hot Chocolate Fudge Sauce

Makes 6

These lovely marbled cakes make a luxurious dessert after a special meal. You could use milk or white chocolate in the sauce, if you prefer.

Prep: 40 mins   Cook: 30 mins

Ingredients

1 tablespoon vegetable oil, for oiling

1 tablespoon flour, for dusting

½ cup vegetable oil

⅔ cup superfine or granulated sugar

¼ cup milk

2 eggs, beaten

1¼ cups all-purpose flour, sifted

1¾ teaspoons baking powder

3 tablespoons unsweetened cocoa powder, sifted

Sauce

1¼ cups heavy cream

8 ounces semisweet chocolate, chopped

1 tablespoon light corn syrup

2 tablespoons butter

1. Lightly oil six ¾-cup dariole molds or ramekin dishes and dust with flour. Preheat the oven to 350°F.

2. Put the oil, sugar, milk, and eggs into a mixing bowl and gently whisk to combine. Divide the mixture between two bowls.

3. Add ¾ cup of the flour and half the baking powder to one of the bowls and fold to combine. Add the remaining flour and baking powder together with the cocoa powder to the other bowl and mix well. Make sure that both batters have the same consistency; they should be pourable but not runny. If they need to be looser, add a little more milk.

4. Begin to build the cake layers in the molds. Pour a little of the vanilla batter into each of the molds to cover the bottom. Pour a little of the chocolate batter into the center of each, then repeat with the vanilla batter. Alternate and repeat until all the batter has been used, always pouring into the center to form a "zebra" pattern. Place the molds on a baking sheet and bake in the preheated oven for 20–25 minutes, until well risen and a toothpick inserted in the middle of the cakes comes out clean. Leave in the molds until ready to serve.

5. Meanwhile, make the sauce. Heat the cream in a saucepan to just below boiling point. Stir in the chocolate, corn syrup, and butter and gently mix until the chocolate has melted and combined with the other ingredients. The sauce should be smooth and glossy.

6. Remove the cakes from the molds, pour the sauce over the cakes, and serve immediately.

CHOCOLATE POLENTA
Cake

Serves 6

A scoop of vanilla ice cream or tangy crème fraîche and a few fresh berries will turn this wonderfully moist and crumbly chocolate cake into a heavenly dessert.

Prep: 15 mins   Cook: 15–20 mins

Ingredients

½ tablespoon butter, for greasing

⅔ cup all-purpose flour

½ teaspoon baking powder

¼ cup unsweetened cocoa powder

⅓ cup instant polenta

1 stick butter, softened

⅔ cup superfine or granulated sugar

2 extra-large eggs

2 tablespoons unsweetened cocoa powder, for dusting

prepared chocolate sauce, to serve (optional)

1. Preheat the oven to 400°F. Grease an 8-inch round shallow cake pan and line the bottom with parchment paper. Sift together the flour, baking powder, and cocoa powder into a large bowl and add the polenta, butter, sugar, and eggs. Beat with a handheld electric mixer for 1–2 minutes, until combined.

2. Spoon the batter into the prepared pan and gently level the surface. Bake in the preheated oven for 15–20 minutes, or until risen and just firm to the touch.

3. Carefully turn out the cake onto a wire rack. Serve warm or cold, cut into thin slices (allow 2 slices per person), dusted with cocoa powder and drizzled with chocolate sauce, if using.

VARIATION

To make a lemon polenta cake, replace the cocoa powder with 1 tablespoon all-purpose flour and add the grated zest and juice of 1 lemon. Bake for 18–24 minutes.

MELT

CHOCOLATE MOUSSE
with a Spicy Kick

Serves 4

These heavenly little desserts have a good undertone of dark rum, zingy orange, and delicious sour cherries, as well as the unexpected spicy kick.

Prep: 20 mins, plus cooling and setting   Cook: 5 mins

Ingredients

6 ounces bittersweet chocolate, broken into pieces

pinch of salt

4 extra-large eggs, separated

¼ cup superfine or granulated sugar

⅔ cup heavy cream

1 teaspoon chipotle powder

2 teaspoons orange zest

⅔ cup dried sour or tart cherries

½ cup dark rum

½ cup hazelnuts, roasted

1. Put the chocolate pieces into a large heatproof bowl set over a saucepan of gently simmering water and heat, stirring occasionally, until melted. Remove from the heat and set aside until cool.

2. Beat the salt, egg yolks, and sugar into the cooled chocolate.

3. In a separate bowl, whip the cream until slightly thickened.

4. Put the egg whites into a clean, grease-free bowl and whisk until they hold stiff peaks.

5. Add the chipotle powder and 1 teaspoon of the orange zest to the chocolate mixture, then fold in the cream, followed by the egg whites. Divide among four glasses and place in the refrigerator for 2 hours to set.

6. Meanwhile, soak the dried cherries in the rum and coarsely chop the hazelnuts.

7. Just before serving, remove the mousse from the refrigerator and top with the rum-soaked dried cherries, the hazelnuts, and the remaining orange zest.

LEMON & WHITE
Chocolate Creams

For an Asian twist on these decadent truffles, add a large pinch of ground cardamom seeds and star anise to the cream and chocolate mixture.

Prep: 40 mins, plus setting   Cook: 5–10 mins

Ingredients

10 ounces white chocolate, coarsely chopped

2 tablespoons heavy cream

finely grated zest of 1 lemon

2 tablespoons limoncello

4 tablespoons unsalted butter, softened and diced

3 tablespoons finely chopped pistachio nuts

1. Put one-third of the chocolate and all the cream into a heatproof bowl set over a saucepan of gently simmering water and heat until the chocolate is melted.

2. Remove from the heat, add the lemon zest, limoncello, and butter and whisk for 3–4 minutes, or until thickened. Transfer to an airtight container and chill in the refrigerator for 6–8 hours, or until firm.

3. Line a baking sheet with nonstick parchment paper. Scoop teaspoonfuls of the mixture and, using the palms of your hands, roll them into 12 truffle-size balls. Place the balls on the prepared baking sheet, cover with plastic wrap, and freeze for 6–8 hours.

4. Put the remaining chocolate into a heatproof bowl set over a saucepan of gently simmering water and heat until melted.

5. Using two forks, dip each truffle into the chocolate to coat evenly. Return to the baking sheet, sprinkle with the pistachio nuts, and chill in the refrigerator for 1–2 hours, or until firm. Store in an airtight container in the refrigerator for up to 5 days.

S'MORES
Semifreddo

Serves 8

Semifreddo is an easy-to-slice ice cream that looks striking and tastes divine. It's a perfect dessert for preparing ahead and impressing at any dinner party or occasion.

Prep: 40 mins, plus chilling   Cook: 10 mins

Ingredients

1 teaspoon vegetable oil, for oiling

4 ounces semisweet chocolate

4 extra-large eggs, separated

½ cup superfine or granulated sugar

1¼ cups heavy cream

1⅔ cups crushed graham crackers, plus 1 graham cracker to decorate

⅔ cup dulce de leche (caramel sauce)

1⅓ cups white mini marshmallows

½ teaspoon water

1. Oil a 9 x 5 x 3-inch loaf pan and line with plastic wrap. Put half the chocolate into a heatproof bowl set over a saucepan of gently simmering water and heat until melted. Remove from the heat.

2. Put the egg yolks and sugar into a separate bowl and whisk until they leave a trail when the whisk or beaters are lifted.

3. Put the egg whites into a clean, grease-free bowl and whisk until they hold stiff peaks. Pour the cream into a separate bowl and whip until it holds soft peaks.

4. Using a large metal spoon, fold the cream into the egg yolk mixture, then fold in the melted chocolate and, finally, carefully fold in the egg whites. Spoon one-third of the mixture into the prepared pan, then sprinkle half the crushed graham crackers over the top. Drizzle with half the dulce de leche, then repeat one time before topping with the remaining egg mixture. Wrap with plastic wrap and transfer to the freezer for at least 6 hours, until firm.

5. To serve, remove from the freezer and set aside while you prepare the toppings. Put the remaining chocolate into a heatproof bowl set over a saucepan of gently simmering water and heat until melted.

6. Put 1 cup of the marshmallows in the microwave with the water and heat for 10–15 seconds on Low. Mix together until smooth and thick but still runny.

7. Remove the plastic wrap from the semifreddo and turn out onto a plate. Spoon the melted marshmallow over it and let dribble down the edges. Sprinkle with the remaining marshmallows and drizzle the chocolate back and forth over the top to achieve a zigzag effect. Crush the remaining cracker, sprinkle the crumbs over the top of the semifreddo, and serve immediately.

TIP

If the dulce de leche is thick when you spoon it onto the semifreddo, it will sink. Heat gently in the microwave, and when it has cooled lightly, drizzle it back and forth over the semifreddo to achieve a more even layer.

MISSISSIPPI
Mud Pie

A sticky chocolate pie that's great with vanilla ice cream, this recipe has homemade pastry for the crust, but you could use leftover cookies for a more traditional crust.

Serves 6–8

Prep: 30 mins, plus cooling   Cook: 35–40 mins

Ingredients

3 ounces semisweet chocolate

6 tablespoons unsalted butter

⅓ cup firmly packed light brown sugar

2 eggs, beaten

½ cup light cream

1 teaspoon vanilla extract

Pastry dough

1⅓ cups all-purpose flour

¼ cup unsweetened cocoa powder

¼ cup firmly packed light brown sugar

6 tablespoons butter

2–3 tablespoons cold water

1 tablespoon flour, for dusting

Topping

1 cup heavy cream

3 ounces semisweet chocolate

1. Preheat the oven to 400°F. To make the dough, sift the flour and cocoa powder into a bowl and stir in the sugar. Rub in the butter with your fingertips until the mixture resembles fine bread crumbs. Add just enough water to bind to a dough.

2. Roll out the dough on a lightly floured work surface to a circle large enough to line a 1¼-inch deep, 8-inch round tart pan. Use the dough to line the pan. Prick the bottom with a fork, cover with a piece of parchment paper, and fill with pie weights or dried beans, then bake in the preheated oven for 10 minutes. Remove from the oven and take out the paper and weights. Reduce the oven temperature to 350°F.

3. Put the chocolate and butter into a saucepan and heat over low heat, stirring, until melted. Put the sugar and eggs into a bowl and whisk together until smooth, then stir in the chocolate mixture, cream, and vanilla extract.

4. Pour the mixture into the pastry shell and bake in the oven for 20–25 minutes or until just set. Let cool.

5. To make the topping, whip the cream until it just holds its shape, then spread over the pie. Put the chocolate into a bowl set over a saucepan of gently simmering water and heat until melted, then spoon into a pastry bag and pipe decorations over the cream. Serve cold.

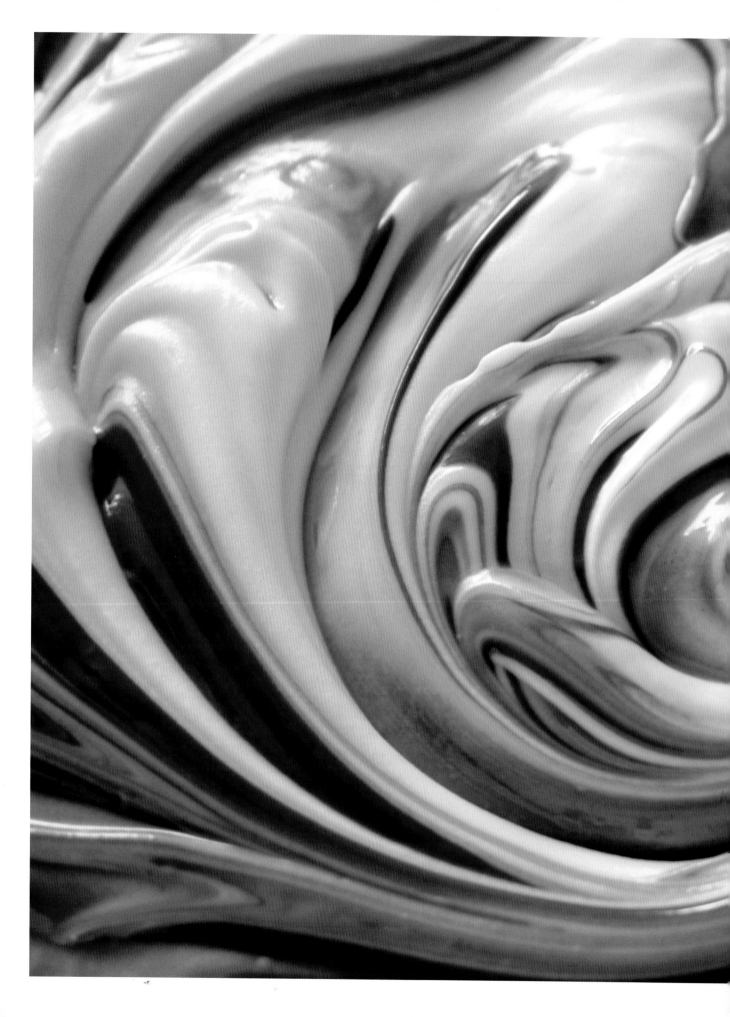

CHOCOLATE
fondue

Prepared in a slow cooker, this easy-to-make yet decadent dessert is a fun way to end a dinner party. Don't prepare the fruit until you're ready to serve the fondue.

Serves 4–6

Prep: 5 mins   Cook: 45–60 mins

Ingredients

½ tablespoon butter, for greasing

1 cup heavy cream

12 ounces semisweet chocolate, chopped into small pieces

1 teaspoon vanilla extract

To Serve

8 ounces strawberries, hulled

2 bananas, peeled and sliced

1 apple, cut into chunks

marshmallows (optional)

1. Grease the inside of a slow cooker. Put the cream and chocolate into the slow cooker and stir to combine. Cover and cook on low, stirring occasionally, for 45–60 minutes, until the chocolate is completely melted. Stir in the vanilla extract.

2. Keep the mixture in the slow cooker or transfer to a fondue pot with a burner and serve immediately, with plates of strawberries, bananas, apple, and marshmallows, if using, for dipping.

CHOCOLATE CHIP COOKIES
& Ice Cream Cake

Serves 8–10

This stunning layered ice cream cake will definitely impress and is well worth the effort of baking three separate cookies. It's delicious, too.

Prep: 30 mins, plus chilling and freezing   Cook: 15 mins

Ingredients

1½ sticks butter, softened

1 cup firmly packed dark brown sugar

½ cup superfine or granulated sugar

1 egg, plus 1 egg yolk

1 teaspoon vanilla extract

2 cups all-purpose flour

½ teaspoon salt

½ teaspoon baking soda

12 ounces semisweet chocolate, broken into pieces

½ tablespoon butter, for greasing

2 quarts vanilla ice cream

1. Using a food processor on high speed, cream together the butter, brown sugar, and superfine sugar for 8 minutes, or until pale and doubled in size. Reduce the speed of the food processor slightly and gradually add the egg, egg yolk, and vanilla extract until well combined. Turn off the food processor and sift in the flour, salt, and baking soda. With the food processor on low, process the mixture until well combined, then add the chocolate and mix briefly. Chill in the refrigerator for 30 minutes.

2. Preheat the oven to 350°F. Grease and line three 9-inch round cake pans, at least one of which should be springform.

3. Remove the dough from the refrigerator and divide into three equal pieces. Press the dough into the bottom of the pans, making sure the thickness of the dough is even and that it goes right to the edges.

4. Cook in the preheated oven, in batches if necessary, for 15 minutes, or until just turning golden. Remove from the oven and let cool in the pans.

5. Meanwhile, remove the ice cream from the freezer to soften.

6. Remove two cookies from their pans. Keep the cookie in the springform pan as the bottom of the cake and build your cake with alternate, equal layers of ice cream and cookie, finishing with the best-looking cookie on top. Push down gently to make sure the ice cream reaches the sides of the pan.

7. Put into the freezer for 4 hours. Remove from the freezer 10 minutes before serving and release and remove the springform. Cut into wedges and serve immediately.

TIP

The chocolate will set quickly in the molds, so be sure to sprinkle the chunks with the toppings as soon as possible after the sticks have been inserted.

CHOCOLATE CHUNK
Sticks

Makes 10–15

Who would have thought that little blocks of chocolate on sticks would bring so much joy? Just dissolve them in hot milk for a perfect hot chocolate drink.

Prep: 5–10 mins, plus setting   Cook: 5–10 mins

Ingredients

8 ounces semisweet chocolate, milk chocolate, or white chocolate, or a mixture, finely chopped

2–4 tablespoons of your choice of:

instant coffee granules

flaked dried coconut

toasted nuts

mini marshmallows

chocolate sprinkles

edible glitter

5 cups low-fat milk or whole milk, to serve

1. Put the chocolate into a heatproof bowl set over a saucepan of gently simmering water and heat until melted. If you are using different chocolates, melt them in separate bowls.

2. Divide the chocolate among silicone molds, a silicone ice cube tray or small paper liners. Let cool slightly until the chocolate begins to thicken, then push a small wooden spoon, lollipop stick, or wooden coffee stirrer into each mold so it stands upright.

3. While the chocolate is still soft, sprinkle each chunk with your choice of toppings, then let set solid.

4. To serve, heat 1 mug of milk for each chocolate chunk stick. Remove any paper liners and stir a stick into each mug of milk until melted. Serve immediately.

Boozy Chocolate
Cheesecake

Serves 8

Cream liqueurs are the perfect ingredient in cheesecakes—they add a decadent yet smooth touch of alcohol to the nation's favorite dessert.

Prep: 30 mins, plus chilling   Cook: 10 mins

Ingredients

1 tablespoon vegetable oil, for oiling

18 chocolate chip cookies (about 6 ounces)

4 tablespoons unsalted butter

crème fraîche or whipped cream and fresh fruit, to serve (optional)

Filling

8 ounces semisweet chocolate, broken into pieces

8 ounces milk chocolate, broken into pieces

¼ cup superfine or granulated sugar

1½ cups cream cheese

2 cups heavy cream, lightly whipped

3 tablespoons Irish cream liqueur

1. Line the bottom of an 8-inch round springform cake pan with parchment paper and brush the sides with oil. Put the cookies into a plastic bag and crush them with a rolling pin. Put the butter into a saucepan and gently heat until melted. Stir in the crushed cookies. Press into the bottom of the prepared pan and chill in the refrigerator for 1 hour.

2. Put the semisweet chocolate and milk chocolate into a heatproof bowl set over a saucepan of gently simmering water and heat until melted. Remove from the heat and let cool. Put the sugar and cream cheese into a bowl and beat together until smooth, then fold in the cream. Fold the melted chocolate into the cream cheese mixture, then stir in the liqueur.

3. Spoon the mixture into the pan and smooth the surface. Let chill in the refrigerator for 2 hours, or until firm. Transfer to a serving plate and cut into slices. Serve with crème fraîche or whipped cream and fresh fruit, if using.

TIP
You could serve this cheesecake with a glass of cream liqueur or a cup of Irish coffee as a treat on a cold day.

Tools

You don't really need high-tech equipment, but a few must-have items will make chocolate easier to handle, produce stunning decorations, and give your cakes and desserts that professional touch.

Chocolate equipment

Melting
Double boiler or a heatproof bowl that sits over a saucepan for melting chocolate over simmering water on the stove
Candy or instant-read thermometer for checking the temperature of melting chocolate

Cooling
Marble slab for spreading and cooling chocolate

Decorating
Graters, coarse and fine
Swivel peeler for shaving curls
Cutters for hearts, flowers, stars, leaves

Piping cone (see box)
Piping tips
Brushes for painting leaves

Lifting
Spatula for spreading chocolate and lifting fragile decorations
Toothpicks for transferring chocolate curls
Tweezers for lifting and arranging delicate decorations

Paper
Parchment paper for piping decorations and spreading chocolate
Wax paper for lifting and transferring chopped chocolate and for making piping cones (see opposite)

Baking equipment

Weighing and measuring
Measuring cups
Measuring spoons

Mixing
Bowls
Handheld electric mixer
Immersion blender
Food processor
Spatula
Wooden spoons

Pastry tools
Rolling pin
Silicone pastry mat
Marble slab
Pastry brush
Dough scraper

Trays and pans
Baking sheet
Madeleine pan
Muffin pan
Cake pans
13 x 9-inch baking pan
Springform cake pans
Tart pans

Papers and liners
Parchment paper
Wax paper
Silicone sheets
Paper cupcake liners
Muffin cups (paper or silicone)

How to make a paper piping cone

- Cut out a square of wax paper approximately 10 x 10 inches. Fold in half diagonally to make two triangles (only one triangle is needed to make the bag).
- Hold the triangle by both corners of the longest side.
- Loop one corner inside the other to form a cone, with the tip of the cone facing away from you.
- Put one hand inside the cone, holding it together between your thumb and index finger.
- With your other hand, wrap the loose outside end around the cone to close up the point.
- Fold the top over to secure the cone.
- Snip off about ½ inch from the tip of the cone, and drop in a piping tip. Otherwise, snip off just a tiny part of the tip and pipe directly from the bag.

Filling and closing the bag
- Stand the cone in a glass. Spoon the chocolate or frosting into the bag to no more than two-thirds full. It will be difficult to handle if you overfill. To close the bag, flatten the cone above the filling and fold over both corners to seal. Keep folding over the top as you pipe.

MOUSSE-AU-CHOCOLAT Tarts

Makes 6

Chocolate mousse is wonderfully creamy, because plenty of air gets in when it is beaten. The flavor depends on the chocolate, so buy the best-quality chocolate that you can.

Prep: 45 mins, plus chilling   Cook: 45 mins

Ingredients

Pastry dough

2 cups all-purpose flour, plus 4 teaspoons for dusting

pinch of salt

¼ cup superfine or granulated sugar

1¼ sticks butter

1 egg

finely grated zest of 1 lemon

Filling

1⅓ cups light cream

12 ounces bittersweet chocolate, broken into pieces

5 egg yolks

¼ cup superfine or granulated sugar

2½ tablespoons water

sea salt flakes, to decorate (optional)

1. Preheat the oven to 350°F. To make the dough, put the flour, salt, sugar, butter, egg, and lemon zest into a bowl and mix together. Roll the dough into a ball, wrap in plastic wrap, and chill for 30 minutes in the refrigerator.

2. Roll out the dough on a lightly floured work surface and ease it into six 4-inch tart pans, then line them with parchment paper and fill with pie weights or dried beans. Bake in the preheated oven for 15 minutes, then remove the weights and paper and bake for an additional 10 minutes.

3. To make the filling, heat the cream in a heatproof bowl set over a saucepan of gently simmering water, then add the chocolate and heat until melted. Remove from the heat and let cool to room temperature.

4. Put the egg yolks, sugar, and water into a separate heatproof bowl set over a saucepan of simmering water and heat, whisking constantly, for 8–10 minutes, until the mixture thickens. Remove from the heat, stir into the chocolate mixture, and beat with a handheld electric mixer for 5–6 minutes.

5. Pour the filling into the pastry shells. Carefully transfer to the refrigerator and chill for 2–3 hours, or until the filling is firm. Serve chilled, decorated with sea salt flakes, if using.

CHOCOLATE BAKED
Alaska

This classic meringue and ice cream combo is a real showstopper. Use a good-quality ice cream that won't melt too quickly and serve as soon as it comes out of the oven.

Prep: 30 mins, plus freezing   Cook: 5 mins

Ingredients

1 quart chocolate ice cream

6 prepared chocolate brownies

2 extra-large egg whites

½ cup superfine or granulated sugar

2 tablespoons unsweetened cocoa powder, for dusting

1. Line a deep 3-cup round baking dish with plastic wrap. Put the ice cream into the baking dish. Slice off any excess ice cream above the rim of the baking dish and cut it into smaller chunks. Push the chunks into the gaps around the main block of ice cream. Top with a layer of the chocolate brownies, cutting to fit, if necessary, and press down firmly. Put into the freezer for 15 minutes.

2. Preheat the oven to 425°F. Put the egg whites into a clean, grease-free bowl and whisk until they hold firm peaks. Gradually whisk in the sugar, a spoonful at a time, to make a firm and glossy meringue.

3. Remove the baking dish from the freezer and turn out onto a baking sheet. Quickly spoon and spread the meringue all over the ice cream and the edge of the chocolate brownie crust to cover completely. Bake in the preheated oven for 5 minutes, or until the meringue is just set and lightly browned. Serve immediately, lightly dusted with cocoa powder.

VARIATION

For individual versions, simply top each brownie with a scoop of the ice cream, then smother in the meringue. Reduce the cooking time to 3-4 minutes.

TIP
If you want perfect ice cream circles, spoon the ice cream into a brownie pan to the thickness you desire. Use a round pastry cutter to cut out sharp circles of ice cream.

CHOCOLATE & TOASTED
Coconut Ice Cream Sandwiches

Makes 4

Take these incredible ice-cream sandwiches further with a little fudge sauce. Remove the top cookies, add a spoon of sauce to the bottom cookies, and replace the tops.

Prep: 30 minutes, plus cooling   Cook: 15 mins

Ingredients

4 tablespoons unsalted butter

¼ cup firmly packed light brown sugar

1½ teaspoons light corn syrup

⅓ cup all-purpose flour

¼ cup unsweetened cocoa powder

2 tablespoons chocolate chips

1 tablespoon flour, for dusting

⅓ cup flaked dried coconut

4 scoops coconut ice cream

1. Preheat the oven to 350°F. Line a baking sheet with parchment paper. Beat together the butter and sugar until pale and fluffy. Add the corn syrup and beat again until combined. Fold in the flour, cocoa powder, and chocolate chips.

2. Bring the dough together on a floured surface and divide into 8 equal portions. Shape each portion into a ball, then flatten the balls slightly with the palm of your hand and place on the prepared baking sheet, spaced well apart to allow for spreading.

3. Transfer to the preheated oven and bake for 10–12 minutes, until set. Let cool on the baking sheet for 5 minutes, then transfer to a wire rack to cool completely.

4. Put the coconut into a heavy skillet over medium heat and cook, stirring, for 1–2 minutes, until lightly golden. Remove from the heat and transfer to a plate to cool.

5. Place a scoop of ice cream on a cookie and, working quickly, spread it into a circle. Sandwich with another cookie on top and gently roll through the toasted coconut. Repeat until you have used all the ice cream and cookies. Serve immediately.

CHOC BERRY
Rockets

Makes 8

Kids can have fun making these tasty iced treats by dipping them into chocolate and edible sprinkles to create their own masterpieces.

Prep: 40 mins, plus cooling and freezing   Cook: 12–15 mins

Ingredients

3¼ cups raspberries

2 tablespoons lemon juice

9 ounces semisweet chocolate, coarsely chopped

½ cup colorful sprinkles

Sugar Syrup

⅓ cup granulated sugar

1 cup water

1. To make the sugar syrup, put the sugar and water into a small saucepan over low heat and heat for 6–8 minutes, until the sugar has dissolved. Increase the heat to high and bring to a boil, then reduce the heat to medium and simmer for 3–4 minutes. Remove from the heat and let cool.

2. Put the raspberries, lemon juice, and sugar syrup in a blender and process until pureed. Press the puree through a fine metal strainer to remove the seeds. Pour into eight ½-cup ice-pop molds. Insert an ice-pop stick into each mold and freeze for 3–4 hours, or until firm.

3. When the raspberry mixture is frozen, line a baking sheet with parchment paper. To unmold the ice pops, dip the frozen molds into warm water for a few seconds and gently release the pops while holding the sticks. Place them on the prepared baking sheet and return to the freezer for 1–2 hours.

4. When the ice pops are frozen, put the chocolate into a heatproof bowl set over a saucepan of gently simmering water and heat until melted. Remove from the heat and let cool slightly.

5. Put the sprinkles onto a sheet of parchment paper. Dip each ice pop into the melted chocolate so it is covered to about halfway up, then roll it in the sprinkles. Return to the prepared baking sheet and freeze for 10–20 minutes, or until ready to serve.

CHOCOLATE FUDGE
Ice Cream

Serves 4–6

Chocolate and fudge are a delicious combination, and they become even more irresistible when combined with rich ice cream.

Prep: 20 mins, plus freezing   Cook: 25 mins

Ingredients

1¼ cups milk

4 ounces semisweet chocolate, broken into pieces

2 tablespoons butter

1 teaspoon vanilla extract

⅔ cup superfine or granulated sugar

⅓ cup light corn syrup

4 eggs

1¼ cups heavy cream

cookies, to serve (optional)

1. Pour ¾ cup of the milk into a heavy saucepan. Add the chocolate, butter, and vanilla extract and gently heat over low heat, stirring constantly. Stir in the sugar and corn syrup and bring to a boil. Reduce the heat and simmer for 4 minutes, without stirring. Remove from the heat.

2. Put the eggs into a bowl and beat well. Add the chocolate mixture, stirring constantly.

3. Return the mixture to the rinsed-out pan and cook over low heat for an additional 10–15 minutes, stirring constantly, until the mixture is thick enough to coat the back of the wooden spoon. Do not let the mixture boil, or it will curdle.

4. Remove the mixture from the heat, add the remaining milk and the cream, and stir together until smooth. Submerge the bottom of the pan into a bowl of ice-cold water to stop the cooking process. Let cool for at least 1 hour, stirring from time to time to prevent a skin from forming.

5. If using an ice-cream maker, churn the mixture following the manufacturer's directions. Alternatively, freeze in a freezer-proof container, uncovered, for 1–2 hours, or until it begins to set around the edges. Turn out into a bowl and stir with a fork until smooth. Return to the container and freeze for an additional 2–3 hours, or until completely frozen.

6. To store, cover the container with a suitable lid. Remove the ice cream from the freezer and put into the refrigerator for 15–20 minutes before serving. Serve with cookies, if using.

TRIPLE CHOCOLATE
Mousses

Makes 36

These impressive desserts can be prepared the day before you plan to serve them. You can even serve them frozen, and they are easier to slice if not fully thawed.

Prep: 45 mins, plus chilling and freezing   Cook: 2 mins

Ingredients

4 tablespoons unsalted butter

1 tablespoon unsweetened cocoa powder

1¼ cups crushed graham crackers

milk chocolate curls, to decorate (optional)

Mousse

¼ cup water

4 teaspoons powdered gelatin

4 ounces semisweet chocolate, coarsely chopped

4 ounces milk chocolate, coarsely chopped

4 ounces white chocolate, coarsely chopped

1 stick unsalted butter

⅓ cup milk

6 eggs, separated

½ teaspoon vanilla extract

1½ cups heavy cream

1. Line a deep 8-inch square, loose-bottom cake pan with two long strips of plastic wrap, laid over each other in a cross, with an overhang on all sides of the pan. Melt the butter in a small saucepan, then stir in the cocoa powder and cookie crumbs. Press the mixture into the pan in an even layer, then cover and chill in the refrigerator.

2. To make the mousse, put the water into a small heatproof bowl, then sprinkle the gelatin over the surface, making sure the powder is absorbed. Set aside for 5 minutes, then set the bowl over a saucepan of gently simmering water and heat for 5 minutes, stirring occasionally, until the gelatin is a clear liquid.

3. Put each type of chocolate into a separate heatproof bowl with one-third of the butter and 2 tablespoons of milk. Put the bowls over saucepans of gently simmering water and heat until the chocolate has melted. Stir 2 egg yolks into each bowl, then remove from the heat. Stir 4 teaspoons of the gelatin into each bowl, then stir the vanilla extract into the white chocolate. Pour the cream into a fourth bowl and whisk until it holds soft peaks. Fold one-third of the cream into each mixture. Whisk the egg whites in a large, clean bowl until they hold soft peaks, then divide them among the chocolate mixtures and fold in gently.

4. Pour the semisweet chocolate mousse into the pan and freeze for 15 minutes. Spoon the white chocolate layer on top and freeze for 30 minutes. Gently whisk the milk chocolate layer to soften, then spoon it on top and chill in the refrigerator overnight, or until set.

5. Lift the mousse out of the pan, pressing from the bottom. Peel off the plastic wrap. Cut the mousse into 6 strips, using a wet knife, then cut each strip into 6 small squares, wiping and wetting the knife often so that the layers don't become smeared. Arrange on small plates and decorate with chocolate curls, if using.

VARIATION

Try substituting the milk with coconut milk or almond milk for a different flavor.

MELTING CHOCOLATE
Risotto

Serves 4–6

Who said risotto can't be sweet? This oozy chocolate dessert is the ultimate comfort food—think of it as a luxury rice pudding.

Prep: 10 mins, plus resting   Cook: 45 mins

Ingredients

1¾ cups milk

2½ tablespoons superfine or granulated sugar

½ cup risotto rice

1 teaspoon vanilla extract

4 ounces semisweet chocolate, broken into small pieces

¼–⅓ cup heavy cream

1. Preheat the oven to 300°F. Put a 1-quart ovenproof dish in the oven to warm.

2. Put the milk, sugar, and rice into a saucepan and bring just to a boil over low heat.

3. Stir through the vanilla extract and two-thirds of the chocolate and stir until the chocolate has melted. Carefully transfer to the dish to the preheated oven. Cover with aluminum foil and bake for 30 minutes.

4. Remove from the oven, stir well, replace the foil, and let rest for 5 minutes. Drizzle with the cream and swirl it into the risotto. Sprinkle with the remaining chocolate to serve.

MELTING CHOCOLATE
Sheet Cake

Serves 12–15

This delicious cake is light in texture and big on sweetness—and, of course, it will be a popular dessert at any small party or informal gathering.

Prep: 30 mins, plus cooling   Cook: 45 mins

Ingredients

½ tablespoon butter, for greasing

1 tablespoon flour, for dusting

2 cups all-purpose flour

2 cups superfine or granulated sugar

¼ cup unsweetened cocoa powder

1 teaspoon baking soda

1 cup water

1 stick butter

½ cup vegetable shortening

½ cup buttermilk

2 eggs

1 teaspoon vanilla extract

Chocolate-Pecan Frosting

1 stick butter

¼ cup unsweetened cocoa powder

⅓ cup milk

⅔ cup confectioners' sugar

1 teaspoon vanilla extract

1 cup pecans, lightly toasted and chopped

1. Preheat the oven to 400°F. Lightly grease a deep 13 x 9-inch baking pan and dust with flour, shaking out any excess.

2. Combine the flour, sugar, cocoa powder, and baking soda in a large mixing bowl, stirring well to combine, then set aside until needed.

3. Combine the water, butter, and shortening in a heavy saucepan and cook over medium heat, stirring constantly with a wire whisk, until the butter is melted. Add the buttermilk, eggs, and vanilla extract and whisk until combined. Pour the chocolate mixture over the flour mixture, stirring well.

4. Pour the batter into the prepared pan and bake in the preheated oven for 25–30 minutes, or until a toothpick inserted in the center of the cake comes out clean. Let cool in the pan.

5. Meanwhile, make the frosting. Combine the butter, cocoa powder, and milk in a medium saucepan and cook over low heat for 5 minutes, or until the butter is melted. Increase the heat to medium and bring to a boil, stirring constantly. Stir in the sugar, vanilla extract, and pecans and beat until smooth and the sugar is dissolved. Spread the frosting over the cooled cake.

TRIPLE CHOCOLATE
Ice Pops

Makes 8

For ultimate indulgence, these ice pops will surely hit all the right buttons with their creamy taste and triple chocolate hit. The pops can be frozen for up to 3 months.

Prep: 15 mins, plus cooling and freezing   Cook: 10 mins

Ingredients

1¼ cups heavy cream

4 ounces semisweet chocolate, coarsely chopped

4 ounces white chocolate, coarsely chopped

4 ounces milk chocolate, coarsely chopped

1. Divide the cream equally among three small saucepans. Put the semisweet chocolate in one of the pans, the white chocolate in another, and the milk chocolate in the third.

2. Place each saucepan over gentle heat and stir until the chocolate has melted and the mixture is smooth. Remove from the heat and let cool for 10–12 minutes.

3. Pour the dark chocolate mixture into eight ¼-cup ice-pop molds. Carefully pour the white chocolate mixture over the semisweet chocolate, then pour the milk chocolate mixture over the white chocolate. Insert the ice pop sticks and freeze for 3–4 hours, or until firm.

4. To unmold the ice pops, dip the frozen molds in lukewarm water for a few seconds, then gently release the pops while holding the sticks.

TIP
To insert ice cream sticks, cover the filled molds with aluminum foil, make a small slit in the center of the foil with a sharp knife, and insert the sticks.

Snap

GOOEY CHOCOLATE
Chip Cookies

Makes 8

Luckily, the country's favorite cookies were invented by chance in 1930, when some small pieces of chocolate accidentally fell into some plain cookie dough.

Prep: 10 mins   Cook: 10–12 mins

Ingredients

½ tablespoon unsalted butter, for greasing

1⅓ cups all-purpose flour, sifted

1 teaspoon baking powder

1 stick unsalted butter, melted

⅓ cup firmly packed light brown sugar

¼ superfine or granulated sugar

½ teaspoon vanilla extract

1 egg, beaten

¾ cup semisweet chocolate chips

1. Preheat the oven to 375°F. Lightly grease two baking sheets.

2. Put all of the ingredients into a large mixing bowl and beat until well combined.

3. Place tablespoons of the dough on the prepared baking sheets, spaced well apart to allow for spreading.

4. Bake in the preheated oven for 10–12 minutes, or until golden brown. Transfer to a wire rack and let cool.

NUTTY PEPPERMINT Bark

Makes 25

Kids and adults alike will love this treat. If you can't get hold of peppermint candy canes, substitute them with any hard mint candy.

Prep: 20 mins, plus setting   Cook: 3–4 mins

Ingredients

7 ounces red-and-white striped peppermint candy canes, broken into pieces

1 pound white chocolate, coarsely chopped

⅓ cup chopped pistachio nuts

½ cup chopped walnuts

1. Line a 12 x 8-inch baking pan with parchment paper.

2. Put the broken candy canes into a large plastic bag and seal tightly. Using a rolling pin, bang the bag until the candy is crushed into small pieces.

3. Put the chocolate into a heatproof bowl set over a saucepan of gently simmering water and heat until melted. Remove from the heat and stir in three-quarters of the candy.

4. Pour the mixture into the prepared pan, smooth the surface with a spatula, and sprinkle with the chopped pistachio nuts and walnuts and the remaining candy. Press down slightly to make sure they stick. Cover with plastic wrap and chill in the refrigerator for 30 minutes, or until firm.

5. Break the bark into small, uneven pieces. Store in an airtight container in a cool, dry place for up to 2 weeks.

VARIATION

Use almond extract instead of vanilla extract to give the almond flavor a kick.

DARK CHOCOLATE &
Sea Salt Almond Biscotti

Makes 36

These twice-baked Italian crunchy cookies are perfect for dunking in coffee or tea for a daytime snack or serving after a meal with a hot beverage.

Prep: 20 mins, plus cooling   Cook: 50 mins

Ingredients

3⅔ cups all-purpose flour

½ cup plus 1 tablespoon unsweetened cocoa powder

1 teaspoon baking powder

1 teaspoon sea salt flakes

1½ cups superfine or granulated sugar

1½ cups slivered almonds, toasted

4 eggs, lightly beaten, plus 2 egg yolks

1½ teaspoons vanilla extract

1 tablespoon flour, for dusting

8 ounces semisweet chocolate, broken into pieces

1. Preheat the oven to 350°F. Line a baking sheet with wax paper. Mix the flour, cocoa powder, baking powder, salt, sugar, and slivered almonds together in a large bowl.

2. Stir in the eggs, egg yolks, and vanilla extract. Mix well and bring together in a soft, smooth dough.

3. With floured hands, shape the dough into two 12-inch logs, place the logs on two separate unlined baking sheets and bake in the preheated oven for 30 minutes, until set on top. Let cool for 10 minutes. Reduce the oven temperature to 300°F.

4. Use a serrated knife to cut each log diagonally into ½-inch thick-slices. Lay the slices on the baking sheets and bake for an additional 20 minutes, turning them over after 10 minutes. Transfer to a wire rack and let cool completely.

5. Meanwhile, put the chocolate into a heatproof bowl set over a saucepan of gently simmering water and heat until melted.

6. Dip the cooled biscotti into the melted chocolate, then transfer them to the prepared baking sheet and let set. Store in an airtight container.

DOUBLE CHOCOLATE &
Cherry Cookies

Makes 30

The sour cherries cut through the richness of the chocolate in these tasty little cookies, but don't be fooled—they are extremely indulgent and calorific.

Prep: 15 mins, plus cooling   Cook: 12–15 mins

Ingredients

2 sticks unsalted butter, softened

⅔ cup superfine or granulated sugar

1 egg yolk, lightly beaten

2 teaspoons vanilla extract

2 cups all-purpose flour

¼ cup unsweetened cocoa powder

pinch of salt

12 ounces bittersweet chocolate, chopped

⅓ cup dried sour cherries

1. Preheat the oven to 375°F. Line two baking sheets with parchment paper.

2. Put the butter and sugar into a bowl and mix well with a wooden spoon, then beat in the egg yolk and vanilla extract. Sift the flour, cocoa powder, and salt into the mixture, add the chocolate and sour cherries, and stir until thoroughly combined.

3. Scoop up tablespoons of the dough and shape into balls. Put them on the prepared baking sheets, spaced well apart, and flatten slightly.

4. Bake in the preheated oven for 12–15 minutes. Let cool on the baking sheets for a few minutes, then transfer to wire racks to cool completely.

TIP
For the best flavor, use bittersweet chocolate with a high percent of cocoa solids.

CHOCOLATE-DIPPED
Pumpkin Seed Brittle

Peanut brittle is given a makeover with crunchy pumpkin seeds, a little semisweet chocolate, and a sprinkling of sea salt.

Makes 10–12

Prep: 10 mins, plus setting   Cook: 30 mins

Ingredients

½ tablespoon butter, for greasing

1½ cups granulated sugar

¼ cup light corn syrup

½ cup cold water

1½ tablespoons butter

¼ teaspoon baking soda

⅔ cup pumpkin seeds, warmed

2 ounces semisweet chocolate, broken into pieces

¼ teaspoon sea salt flakes

1. Lightly grease a large, heavy-duty baking sheet. Line a board with parchment paper. Put the sugar, corn syrup, and water into a large, heavy saucepan and heat gently, stirring with a wooden spoon, until the sugar has dissolved. Stir in the butter and heat until melted.

2. Bring the mixture to a boil, without stirring, then cover and boil for 2–3 minutes. Uncover and clip a candy thermometer to the side of the pan. Continue to boil the mixture steadily, without stirring, until it reaches 310°F (the "hard crack" stage) on the thermometer—this will take about 25 minutes.

3. Remove the pan from the heat and stir in the baking soda and pumpkin seeds (be careful, because the mixture may bubble up). Slowly pour the mixture onto the prepared baking sheet, spreading it out to a 12-inch square with a spatula.

4. Let stand for a few minutes, until the brittle is beginning to set, then mark out about 10 thin strips with a greased long-bladed knife. Let stand in a cool place until completely cold and set.

5. Put the chocolate into a small heatproof bowl set over a saucepan of gently simmering water and heat until melted. Remove from the heat and stir until smooth, then let cool for 10 minutes.

6. Using a sharp knife, cut the brittle into long, thin strips (some strips may break into shorter pieces). Dip one end of each piece of brittle in the melted chocolate. Place on the prepared board and sprinkle the chocolate with a few sea salt flakes. Let stand in a cool place until set.

TIP
Don't boil the mixture too rapidly or it may burn and stick to the bottom of the saucepan.

DARK & WHITE
Chocolate Thins

Makes 40

These simple treats are perfect for kids to make. They're also ideal for putting into a pretty box and giving as a present.

Prep: 30 mins, plus setting   Cook: 5–10 mins

Ingredients

Spicy Dark Chocolate Thins

8 ounces semisweet chocolate, coarsely chopped

large pinch of hot chili powder

edible glitter, to decorate (optional)

Cardamom White Chocolate Thins

8 ounces white chocolate, coarsely chopped

½ teaspoon cardamom seeds, crushed

3 tablespoons finely chopped pistachio nuts

chopped pistachio nuts and edible glitter, to decorate (optional)

1. Line four baking sheets with foil petit four liners.

2. For the spicy dark chocolate thins, put the semisweet chocolate into a heatproof bowl set over a saucepan of gently simmering water and heat until melted. Remove from the heat and stir in the chili powder.

3. Drop teaspoons of the chocolate mixture into half of the petit four liners. Sprinkle with a little edible glitter before the chocolate sets, if using. Let set in a cool place, but not in the refrigerator, for 1–2 hours.

4. For the cardamom white chocolate thins, put the white chocolate into a heatproof bowl set over a saucepan of gently simmering water and heat until melted. Remove from the heat and stir in the cardamom and the pistachio nuts.

5. Drop teaspoons of the white chocolate mixture into the remaining petit four liners. Sprinkle with some chopped pistachio nuts and a little edible glitter, if using, before the chocolate sets. Let set in a cool place, but not in the refrigerator, for 1–2 hours. Store in an airtight container in a cool, dry place for up to 5 days.

TIP
If you don't have petit four liners, drop teaspoons of the mixture onto baking sheets lined with nonstick parchment paper.

VARIATION

Invent your own combo with your favorite nuts, dried fruit, or even candies! Or try swapping the chocolate crispies for flavored ones, such as coffee, mint, or orange.

BANANA CHOCOLATE Slab

Make a unique gift for friends by preparing a delicious chocolate slab. It just seems a shame to break something so beautiful.

Makes 1

Prep: 15 mins, plus setting   Cook: 10 mins

Ingredients

8 ounces milk chocolate, finely chopped

8 ounces semisweet chocolate, finely chopped

8 ounces white chocolate, finely chopped

¾ cup dried banana chips

2 ounces fudge pieces

1 tablespoon chocolate flavored rice cereal

1. Line an 8½ x 10½-inch baking pan with wax paper. Put the milk chocolate, semisweet chocolate, and white chocolate into separate heatproof bowls set over saucepans of gently simmering water and heat until melted. Let cool for 1–2 minutes.

2. Working quickly, pour the milk chocolate into the left side of the prepared pan, then pour the white chocolate into the right side of the pan. Pour the semisweet chocolate into the center.

3. Using a knife, carefully drag the different chocolates into each other to create a swirled effect. Sprinkle with the banana chips, fudge pieces, and chocolate crispies. Let set in a cool place for approximately 3 hours, until set hard. Do not chill.

WHITE CHOCOLATE & Macadamia Nut Cookies

Makes 16

These chunky chocolate and nut cookies are quick and easy to make, and they'll soon become a family favorite.

Prep: 25 mins   Cook: 12–14 mins

Ingredients

½ tablespoon butter, for greasing

1 stick butter, softened

½ cup firmly packed light brown sugar

1 tablespoon light corn syrup

1⅓ cups all-purpose flour

1¼ teaspoons baking powder

⅓ cup coarsely chopped macadamia nuts

2 ounces white chocolate, chopped into chunks

1. Preheat the oven to 350°F. Grease two large baking sheets.

2. Put the butter and sugar into a bowl and beat together until pale and creamy, then beat in the corn syrup. Sift in the flour and baking powder, add the nuts, and mix to a coarse dough.

3. Divide the dough into 16 even pieces, shape each piece into a ball, and place the balls on the prepared baking sheet, spaced well apart to allow for spreading. Slightly flatten each ball with your fingertips and top with the chocolate chunks, lightly pressing them into the dough.

4. Bake in the preheated oven for 12–14 minutes, or until the cookies are just set and pale golden. Let them cool on the baking sheets for 5 minutes, then transfer to a wire rack to cool completely.

TIP
If the cookies have spread during baking, reshape them with a knife when they come out of the oven.

DARK CHOCOLATE BAR
with Dried Cherries & Hazelnuts

Makes 16

Rich dark chocolate, dried fruit, and crunchy hazelnuts make this bar a really special treat for morning coffee or an afternoon snack.

Prep: 15 mins, plus chilling   Cook: 10 mins

Ingredients

½ cup dried cherries

½ cup chopped hazelnuts

12 ounces semisweet chocolate, chopped

½ cup crispy rice cereal

1. Line an 11 x 9-inch baking pan with parchment paper. Combine the cherries and hazelnuts in a small bowl and mix well.

2. Put the chocolate into a heatproof bowl set over a saucepan of gently simmering water and heat until melted. Remove from the heat and stir in the rice cereal.

3. Pour the chocolate mixture into the prepared pan and smooth it into a thin layer with a rubber spatula. Immediately top with the cherries and nuts, sprinkling them evenly over the top and pressing them into the chocolate with the palm of your hand. Chill in the refrigerator for at least 1 hour until completely set.

4. Break into pieces and serve at room temperature.

CHOCOLATE FUDGE BROWNIE
Quinoa Cookies

Makes 26

Quinoa flour is made by grinding quinoa seeds and is a great grain- and gluten-free alternative to wheat flours.

Prep: 30 mins, plus cooling   Cook: 12–14 mins

Ingredients

¼ cup coconut oil

4 ounces bittersweet chocolate, broken into pieces

⅓ cup plus 1 tablespoon quinoa flour

1 tablespoon unsweetened cocoa powder

1 teaspoon baking soda

½ teaspoon ground cinnamon

2 eggs

⅔ cup firmly packed light brown sugar

1 teaspoon vanilla extract

1. Preheat the oven to 375°F. Line three baking sheets with nonstick parchment paper.

2. Put the oil and chocolate into a bowl set over a saucepan of gently simmering water and heat for 5 minutes, or until the chocolate has melted, then stir to mix.

3. Put the flour, cocoa powder, baking soda, and cinnamon into a separate bowl and stir together.

4. Put the eggs, sugar, and vanilla extract into a large mixing bowl and whisk together until thick and frothy. Gently fold in the oil-and-chocolate mixture, then add the flour mixture and stir until smooth.

5. Drop tablespoonfuls of the dough on the prepared baking sheets, spaced well apart, then bake in the preheated oven for 7–9 minutes, until crusty and cracked, and still slightly soft to the touch. Let cool and harden slightly on the baking sheets, then lift off the paper and pack into an airtight container. Eat within 3 days.

TIP

To ensure a nice clean edge, keep the squares in the pan when you pour over the white chocolate and drizzle over the semisweet chocolate.

WHITE CHOCOLATE &
Lemon Squares

Makes 9

Tangy lemon squares drenched in creamy white chocolate make the perfect afternoon or after-dinner treat.

Prep: 20 mins, plus cooling and setting   Cook: 45–50 mins

Ingredients

½ tablespoon butter, for greasing

1 stick unsalted butter

1 cup granulated sugar

1 cup all-purpose flour, plus 2 tablespoons

pinch of salt

½ teaspoon vanilla extract

3 eggs

1 tablespoon lemon zest

½ cup lemon juice

4 ounces white chocolate

1 ounce semisweet chocolate

9 fresh raspberries

1. Preheat the oven to 350°F. Grease an 8-inch square baking pan and line with parchment paper.

2. Put the butter, ¼ cup of the sugar, the flour, and salt into a food processor and pulse until fine and grainy. Add the vanilla extract and pulse until the mixture comes together.

3. Turn out into the prepared pan and press down evenly with the back of a spoon. Transfer to the preheated oven and bake for 16–18 minutes, until lightly browned.

4. Meanwhile, whisk together the eggs, the remaining sugar, the lemon zest, lemon juice, and the remaining 2 tablespoons of flour until smooth and combined. Pour over the cake and return to the oven for 30 minutes, until the filling is set. Let cool in the pan.

5. Put the white chocolate into a heatproof bowl set over a saucepan of gently simmering water and heat until melted. Let cool slightly before pouring over the cake. Let set.

6. Put the semisweet chocolate into a separate heatproof bowl set over a saucepan of gently simmering water and heat until melted. Drizzle over the cake. Let set, then cut the cake into squares, place a raspberry on top of each square, and serve.

MINI CRANBERRY &
Ginger Florentines

These crisp, chewy bites are an Italian classic and make a marvelous present at Christmas—or any time of the year.

Makes 48

Prep: 30 mins, plus cooling and setting   Cook: 15–20 mins

Ingredients

½ tablespoon butter,
for greasing

1 tablespoon flour, for dusting

⅓ cup firmly packed
light brown sugar

¼ cup honey

1 stick unsalted butter

¾ cup flaked dried coconut

¾ cup slivered almonds

1 tablespoon finely chopped
candied peel

1 tablespoon finely chopped
crystallized ginger

⅔ cup dried cranberries

⅓ cup all-purpose flour

8 ounces semisweet chocolate,
coarsely chopped

1. Preheat the oven to 350°F. Lightly grease four 12-cup mini muffin pans (the bottom of each cup should be ¾ inch in diameter), then lightly dust with flour.

2. Put the sugar, honey, and butter into a heavy saucepan. Heat gently, stirring, until the sugar has dissolved, tilting the pan to mix the ingredients together. Stir in the coconut, almonds, candied peel, crystallized ginger, cranberries, and flour.

3. Put small teaspoons of the dough into the prepared pans. Bake in the preheated oven for 10–12 minutes, or until golden brown. Let cool in the pans for 1 hour. Using a spatula, transfer to a wire rack and let rest until firm.

4. Meanwhile, put the chocolate into a heatproof bowl set over a saucepan of gently simmering water and heat until melted.

5. Dip each florentine into the melted chocolate so that the bottom is covered. Place on a wire rack, chocolate side up, and let set for 1 hour. Store in an airtight container in a cool, dry place for up to 2 days.

SNAP

Master the techniques of chocolate decoration and you'll be able to transform an ordinary cake or dessert into something really special.

Piping

If you have a steady hand, pipe directly onto the surface. If it's your first time, trace your chosen pattern onto a piece of paper. Place the pattern under a sheet of nonstick parchment paper and tape it securely in place.

If using a tip, insert it in the piping cone; otherwise pipe from the tip of the cone. Fill the cone halfway with melted chocolate and fold over the top.

Using gentle pressure, pipe onto the paper, following the tracing. Point the cone upward when you finish to prevent any chocolate from leaking out.

Let chill, then carefully move into place with a spatula.

Tempering chocolate

Tempering chocolate stabilizes the crystals, making it glossy and easier to mold when making decorations. The simplest method is to melt the chocolate in a bowl set over gently simmering water, then put the bowl in a larger bowl of cold water and stir to cool. Using a candy thermometer, reheat as follows:

Semisweet chocolate: Melt to 104–113°F, cool to 80–82°F, reheat to 89–90°F.

Milk chocolate: Melt to 90°F, cool to 80–82°F, reheat to 86°F.

White chocolate: Melt to 87°F, cool to 80°F, reheat to 82°F.

Curls and shavings

Curls are made from room-temperature chocolate; shavings from chilled chocolate. Using a swivel peeler, shave the sides of the chocolate. Depending on the temperature, curls or shavings will fall from the block. Avoid touching them with your fingers; use a spatula to move them.

Caraque and cones

Pour melted chocolate onto a marble slab or chilled baking sheet, spreading evenly with a spatula. For caraque, hold a long knife at a 45-degree angle, and push the knife away from you, scraping into the chocolate so thin shavings roll up into a cylinder. For cones, position the knife tip securely and scrape in a circular motion.

Leaves

Use pesticide-free, nonpoisonous plant leaves with short stems; stiff, shiny ones, such as citrus or rose, are best. Wash and pat dry thoroughly. Paint a thick layer of melted chocolate onto the veined side. Place the coated leaves on a baking sheet lined with nonstick parchment paper. Let stand in a cool room until completely set. Holding the stem, carefully pull the leaf away from the chocolate. Use a small spatula or tweezers to arrange on a cake.

CHOCOLATE & OAT Cookies

Makes 15

All the goodness of oats, combined with all the luscious sweetness of chocolate-hazelnut spread and the crunchiness of hazelnuts in one delicious little morsel.

Prep: 5 mins, plus cooling   Cook: 15 mins

Ingredients

½ tablespoon butter,
for greasing

6 tablespoons unsalted butter

1 cup chocolate-hazelnut
spread

2 cups rolled oats

¾ cup blanched hazelnuts,
chopped

1. Preheat the oven to 400°F. Grease a baking sheet.

2. Place the butter and chocolate-hazelnut spread into a saucepan and heat gently until just melted.

3. Add the oats and hazelnuts to the chocolate mixture and stir to combine thoroughly.

4. Shape the mixture into 15 equal balls, then press onto the prepared baking sheet. Bake in the preheated oven for 10–12 minutes. Remove from the oven and let rest until firm, then transfer to a wire rack to cool completely.

PEANUT BUTTER
S'mores

Serves 1–2

These delicious little mouthfuls are traditional campout treats, but they are far too wonderful to keep for those summer nights around the campfire.

Prep: 5 mins, plus cooling   Cook: 5 mins

Ingredients

½ cup smooth peanut butter

6 graham crackers

3 ounces semisweet chocolate, broken into squares

1. Preheat the broiler to high. Spread the peanut butter on one side of each graham cracker.

2. Place the chocolate pieces on four of the graham crackers and invert the remaining graham crackers on top.

3. Toast the s'mores under the preheated broiler for about 1 minute, until the filling starts to melt. Turn carefully using tongs. Let cool slightly, then serve.

VARIATION

For a change of pace, you can use gingersnaps or other cookies, which will work just as well.

TIP
Don't touch the caramel—it's hot. And keep watch—it can suddenly brown and burn.

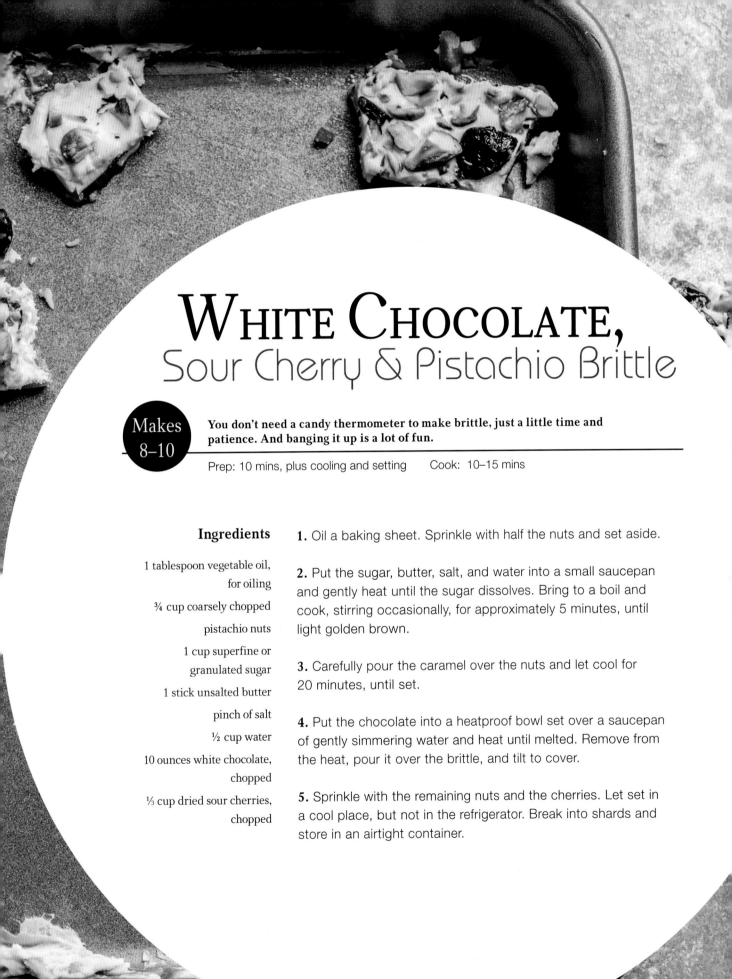

White Chocolate,
Sour Cherry & Pistachio Brittle

Makes 8–10

You don't need a candy thermometer to make brittle, just a little time and patience. And banging it up is a lot of fun.

Prep: 10 mins, plus cooling and setting   Cook: 10–15 mins

Ingredients

1 tablespoon vegetable oil, for oiling

¾ cup coarsely chopped pistachio nuts

1 cup superfine or granulated sugar

1 stick unsalted butter

pinch of salt

½ cup water

10 ounces white chocolate, chopped

⅓ cup dried sour cherries, chopped

1. Oil a baking sheet. Sprinkle with half the nuts and set aside.

2. Put the sugar, butter, salt, and water into a small saucepan and gently heat until the sugar dissolves. Bring to a boil and cook, stirring occasionally, for approximately 5 minutes, until light golden brown.

3. Carefully pour the caramel over the nuts and let cool for 20 minutes, until set.

4. Put the chocolate into a heatproof bowl set over a saucepan of gently simmering water and heat until melted. Remove from the heat, pour it over the brittle, and tilt to cover.

5. Sprinkle with the remaining nuts and the cherries. Let set in a cool place, but not in the refrigerator. Break into shards and store in an airtight container.

GRASSHOPPER MINT
Chocolate Bark

Makes 18–20

This mint-flavored chocolate bark is simple to make but looks amazing and tastes wonderful, too. Break it into shards and serve as an after-dinner treat.

Prep: 20 mins, plus cooling and chilling   Cook: 20 mins

Ingredients

vegetable oil, for oiling

12 ounces semisweet chocolate, broken into pieces

10 ounces white chocolate, broken into pieces

1½ teaspoons peppermint extract

1 teaspoon green liquid food coloring

1. Lightly oil a 13 x 9-inch baking pan and line the bottom and sides with parchment paper.

2. Put the semisweet chocolate into a heatproof bowl set over a saucepan of gently simmering water and heat until melted. Remove from the heat and stir until smooth. Set aside ¼ cup of the melted chocolate in a small, heatproof bowl.

3. Pour the remaining melted chocolate into the prepared pan and gently level the surface with a spatula. Firmly tap the pan on a work surface to remove any air bubbles. Let stand for 15 minutes, or until the pan is cool, then chill in the refrigerator for 30–40 minutes, or until firmly set.

4. Put the white chocolate into a separate heatproof bowl set over a saucepan of gently simmering water and heat until melted. Remove from the heat, let cool for 5–10 minutes, then beat in the peppermint extract and food coloring. The chocolate will start to thicken, but continue beating for 1–2 minutes, until it has a smooth and spreadable consistency.

5. Spoon the mint-flavored chocolate over the set chocolate and spread quickly with a spatula (don't worry if the semisweet chocolate underneath melts slightly). If necessary, remelt the reserved semisweet chocolate by placing the bowl over a saucepan of gently simmering water. Drizzle it over the mint chocolate layer and lightly drag a fork through to create a swirled effect.

6. Chill in the refrigerator for an additional 40–50 minutes, or until the bark is firmly set. Remove from the pan, peel off the paper, and break into chunks to serve.

TIP
For an extra minty flavor, coarsely crush 2–3 pieces of mint candy and sprinkle over the top of the bark before it sets.

STRAWBERRY & WHITE
Chocolate Napoleons

Makes 8

These beautiful treats may look light and airy, but appearances can be deceptive—they are both rich and delicious and will make any occasion special.

Prep: 40 mins, plus cooling and chilling   Cook: 6–8 mins

Ingredients

6 sheets frozen phyllo pastry, thawed

4–6 sprays cooking oil spray

1½ teaspoons superfine or granulated sugar

1 pound fresh strawberries, hulled and sliced

2 tablespoons confectioners' sugar, to decorate

Filling

4 ounces white chocolate, chopped

⅓ cup plus ½ cup water

⅔ cup superfine or granulated sugar

3 egg whites

¼ teaspoon cream of tartar

1. Preheat the oven to 350°F and line a large baking sheet with parchment paper. Carefully separate one phyllo sheet from the others, lay it on a work surface, and spray it all over with the cooking spray. Sprinkle with about ¼ teaspoon of the superfine sugar. Lay another sheet of phyllo on top and repeat the steps until you have three layers. Cut the stack of phyllo sheets into 12 squares and transfer to the prepared baking sheet. Repeat with the remaining three sheets of phyllo pastry so that you have 24 squares. Bake in the preheated oven for 6–8 minutes, until lightly colored. Let cool completely on the baking sheet.

2. To make the filling, put the white chocolate and the ⅓ cup of water into a heatproof bowl set over a saucepan of gently simmering water and heat, stirring frequently, until the chocolate has melted and the mixture is smooth. Set aside.

3. In a small saucepan, combine the sugar with the remaining water and bring to a boil. Cook, stirring, for about 5 minutes or until the mixture begins to thicken.

4. Whisk the egg whites in a large bowl until foamy. Add the cream of tartar and beat for an additional 3 minutes, gradually increasing the speed, until they hold soft peaks. Slowly beat in the warm sugar mixture, then beat on high until the mixture holds stiff, glossy peaks. Whisk one-third of the egg white mixture into the melted chocolate until well combined. Whisk in the remaining egg white mixture. Transfer the mixture to a bowl, cover, and chill in the refrigerator for at least 1 hour.

5. Just before serving, lay eight phyllo squares on the work surface. Top each with about 2 tablespoons of the white chocolate mousse, then top each stack with four to five strawberry slices and another square of phyllo. Repeat with another layer of mousse and strawberries. Finish with a phyllo square and a dusting of confectioners' sugar. Serve immediately.

DISSOLVE

MOLTEN-CENTERED
Chocolate Cupcakes

Makes 8

These luxurious cupcakes, with their gooey melted-chocolate centers, are the ultimate in sweet indulgence. For the best results, use a really good-quality chocolate.

Prep: 20 mins, plus cooling   Cook: 20 mins

Ingredients

⅔ cup all-purpose flour

½ teaspoon baking powder

1 tablespoon unsweetened cocoa powder

4 tablespoons butter, softened

¼ cup superfine or granulated sugar

1 extra-large egg

2 ounces semisweet chocolate

1 tablespoon confectioners' sugar, for dusting

1. Preheat the oven to 375°F and put eight paper liners into a muffin pan.

2. Sift the flour, baking powder, and cocoa powder into a large bowl. Add the butter, superfine sugar, and egg and beat with a handheld electric mixer until smooth.

3. Spoon half of the batter into the paper liners. Using a teaspoon, make an indentation in the center of each. Break the chocolate into 8 pieces and put a piece into each indentation, then spoon the remaining cake batter on top.

4. Bake in the preheated oven for 20 minutes, or until risen and firm to the touch. Let the cupcakes cool in the pan for 2–3 minutes, then serve warm, dusted with the confectioners' sugar.

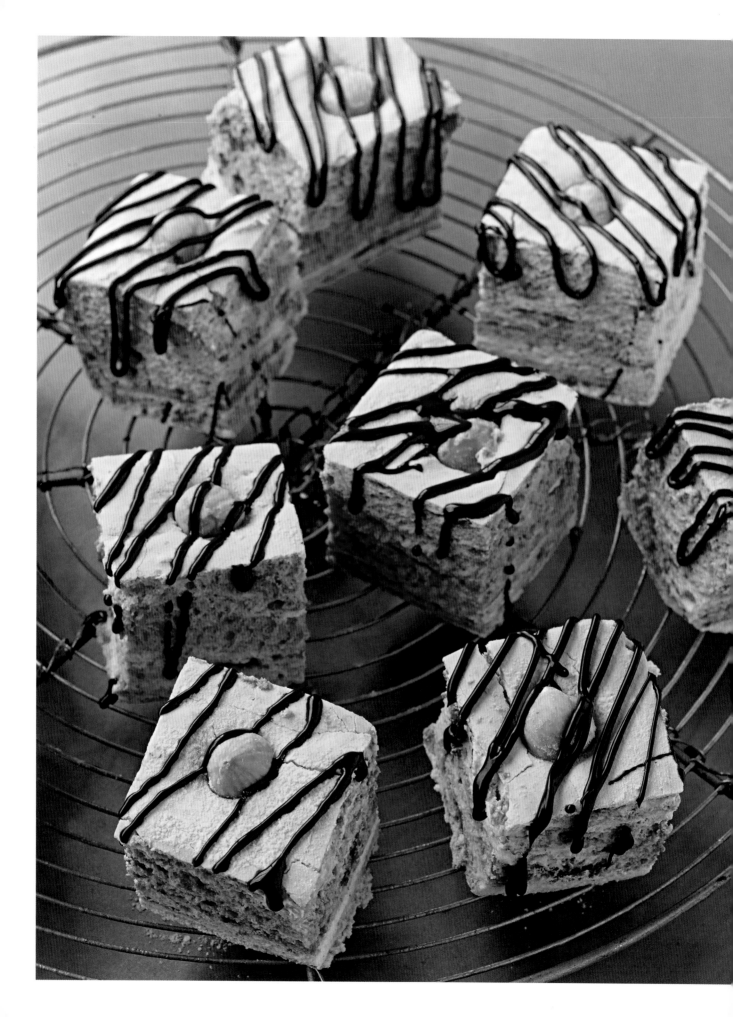

CHOCOLATE & HAZELNUT
Marshmallows

Makes 25

These elegant little treats combine creamy chocolate-hazelnut spread, crunchy toasted hazelnuts, and dreamy marshmallow.

Prep: 45 mins, plus cooling and setting   Cook: 25 mins

Ingredients

1 tablespoon sunflower oil, for oiling

1 tablespoon cornstarch

1 tablespoon confectioners' sugar

25 large marshmallows

3 tablespoons chocolate-hazelnut spread, warmed

25 blanched hazelnuts, toasted

4 ounces semisweet chocolate, broken into pieces, to decorate

1. Lightly oil an 8-inch square shallow cake pan. Line the bottom and two sides with parchment paper, then lightly oil the paper.

2. Sift the cornstarch and confectioners' sugar into a bowl. Use this mixture to dust the lined pan, tapping it firmly so that the mixture coats the bottom and sides completely.

3. Put the marshmallows into a large saucepan with a little water and heat over medium heat, stirring constantly, for 8–10 minutes, or until melted. Gently fold in the warmed chocolate-hazelnut spread.

4. Pour the mixture into the prepared pan and gently level the surface. Lightly dust the top with some of the constarch and sugar mixture, then arrange the hazelnuts evenly on top of the marshmallow. Let set, uncovered, in a cool, dry place for 4–5 hours.

5. Run the tip of a lightly oiled knife along the unlined sides of the pan to release the marshmallow. Using the lining paper, gently lift out the marshmallow and place on a cutting board. Cut into 25 squares, wiping and regreasing the knife frequently. Dust the marshmallows with the cornstarch and sugar mixture.

6. To decorate, put the chocolate into a heatproof bowl set over a saucepan of gently simmering water and heat until melted. Remove from the heat and stir until smooth. Let cool for 10 minutes. Spoon the chocolate into a paper pastry bag and snip off the end. Pipe lines of chocolate over the marshmallows. Let stand in a cool place to set. Store in an airtight container for up to 5 days.

TIP
For a luxurious treat, serve the meringues with whipped cream.

CHOCOLATE & ORANGE
Swirl Meringues

These are the kind of huge meringues you gaze at through a gourmet store window. However, they are easy to make, and you'll be the envy of all your friends.

Makes 8

Prep: 20 mins, plus cooling   Cook: 1 hour 15 mins

Ingredients

½ cupoz blood orange juice

2 tablespoons superfine sugar

1½ tablespoons triple sec

2–4 drops of red food coloring

3 ounces semisweet chocolate, broken into small pieces

Meringues

6 egg whites

1¾ cups superfine sugar

2 teaspoons cornstarch

2 teaspoons white wine vinegar

1. Preheat the oven to 250°F. Line a large baking sheet with parchment paper or a silicone sheet. Place the orange juice, sugar, triple sec, and food coloring in a small saucepan and bring to a boil over medium heat. Boil for 10 minutes, until thick and syrupy. Set aside to cool slightly.

2. Put the chocolate into a heatproof bowl set over a saucepan of gently simmering water and heat until melted. Let cool for 10 minutes.

3. To make the meringues, put the egg whites into a large bowl and whisk until they hold soft peaks. Add the sugar, a tablespoon at a time, whisking after each addition. (If you don't have superfine sugar, you can make it by processing the same amount of granulated sugar in a food processor for 1 minute.) Add the cornstarch and vinegar and continue to whisk until the meringue is thick and glossy and holds stiff peaks.

4. Drizzle half the chocolate over the meringue, then drizzle with half the syrup. Spoon half the egg mixture onto the prepared baking sheet in four large mounds.

5. Drizzle the remaining chocolate and syrup over the remaining meringue mixture in the bowl and spoon out four more large meringues onto the baking sheet. Transfer to the preheated oven and bake for 1 hour. Turn off the oven, open the oven door slightly, and let the meringues cool in the oven.

DARK CHOCOLATE
Roulade

A roulade—or roll—is always an impressive dessert. The contrasting white and dark chocolate and bright-red raspberry drizzle makes this one a work of art.

Serves 6–8

Prep: 45 mins   Cook: 15–20 mins

Ingredients

½ tablespoon butter, for greasing

6 ounces semisweet chocolate, broken into squares

4 extra-large eggs, separated

⅔ cup superfine sugar

2 tablespoons unsweetened cocoa powder, sifted, for dusting

8 ounces white chocolate, broken into squares

1 cup mascarpone cheese

10 tablespoon confectioners' sugar, for sprinkling

Raspberry Coulis

2½ cups raspberries

2 tablespoons confectioners' sugar

1. Preheat the oven to 350°F. Grease a 13 x 9-inch baking pan and line with parchment paper.

2. Put the semisweet chocolate into a heatproof bowl set over a saucepan of gently simmering water and heat until melted. Remove from the heat and let cool slightly.

3. Put the egg yolks and sugar into a bowl and whisk until pale and thick. Whisk the egg whites in a separate, grease-free bowl until they hold soft peaks. Quickly stir the melted chocolate into the egg yolk mixture, then fold in the whisked egg whites. Spread the mixture in the prepared pan and bake in the preheated oven for 15–20 minutes, until risen and firm. Dust a sheet of wax paper with the cocoa powder. Turn out the cake onto the paper, cover with a clean dish towel, and let cool.

4. Meanwhile, put the white chocolate into a heatproof bowl set over a saucepan of gently simmering water and heat until melted. Remove from the heat and let cool slightly. Stir into the mascarpone cheese, mixing until it has a spreadable consistency.

5. Uncover the cake, remove the wax paper, and spread with the white chocolate cream. Use the paper to roll up the cake to enclose the filling (do not worry if it cracks).

6. To make the raspberry coulis, put the raspberries and sugar into a food processor and process to a smooth puree. Press through a fine-mesh strainer to remove the seeds.

7. Sprinkle the cake with confectioners' sugar and serve in slices with the raspberry coulis poured over them.

CHOCOLATE Fritters

These folded triangles can be filled with a variety of ingredients, typically cooked leftovers, and then deep-fried. Here, they've been turned into a delightful dessert.

Makes 16

Prep: 1 hour, plus chilling   Cook: 10–15 mins

Ingredients

1 cup heavy cream

1½ cups semisweet chocolate chips

2 cups all-purpose flour

4 tablespoons butter, melted

oil, for deep-frying

1. Put the cream into a small saucepan and bring to a boil over medium heat. Put the chocolate chips into a bowl, pour the boiling cream over them, and stir until melted. Chill in the refrigerator for 1 hour.

2. Meanwhile, sift the flour into a mixing bowl, add the melted butter, and rub it in. If the dough is too stiff, gradually add a little cold water. Keep covered with a damp cloth.

3. Divide the dough into 16 equal pieces and roll out each piece into a long rectangle. Put 1 teaspoon of the filling onto one end of each rectangle and fold over the dough repeatedly to make a triangle shape.

4. Heat enough oil for deep-frying in a large saucepan to 350–375°F, or until a cube of bread browns in 30 seconds. Add the fritters, in batches if necessary, and cook over medium heat until crisp and golden. Do not overcrowd the pan, and be sure that the oil is brought back to the correct temperature in between each batch. Drain on paper towels and let cool for 5 minutes. Serve warm.

CHOCOLATE & CHERRY
Sorbet

Serves 4

The chocolate makes this sorbet rich and thick, while the frozen cherries add instant glamour.

Prep: 10 mins, plus freezing and softening   Cook: 10 mins

Ingredients

1¼ cups cold water

3 tablespoons stevia (sugar substitute)

¼ cup unsweetened cocoa powder

¼ teaspoon ground allspice

4 cherries, pitted and chopped, plus 4 whole cherries to decorate

2½ ounces good-quality bittersweet chocolate, broken into small pieces

1. Pour the water into a saucepan, then add the stevia, cocoa powder, allspice, and chopped cherries. Lightly whisk together, then slowly bring to a boil over medium-high heat.

2. Remove from the heat and let cool for 2–3 minutes. Stir in the chocolate. Pour the mixture into a freezer-proof container, cover with a lid, and freeze for 4 hours, or until set. Stir with a fork every 30 minutes to break up the ice crystals. Put the whole cherries in the freezer.

3. Take the sorbet out of the freezer 10 minutes before you serve to let it soften. Scoop it into glasses or small bowls, decorate each with a frozen cherry, and serve immediately.

VARIATION
Frozen raspberries would make a good alternative to the cherries in this sorbet. Add them with the chocolate in Step 3.

TIP
Save old jars or bottles
and fill with the fudge
to make delicious
homemade gifts.

HOMEMADE CHOCOLATE
Fudge Sauce

Makes 2½ cups

This simple sauce is your new best friend. Keep a jar in the refrigerator to pair with ice cream, to drizzle on pancakes, or to use in baking.

Prep: 10 minutes, plus cooling   Cook: 10 mins

Ingredients

¾ cup heavy cream

¾ cup light corn syrup

⅓ cup firmly packed
dark brown sugar

½ cup unsweetened
cocoa powder

¼ teaspoon salt

6 ounces semisweet chocolate

2 tablespoons butter

1 teaspoon vanilla extract

1. Put the cream, corn syrup, sugar, cocoa powder, salt, and half the chocolate into a medium saucepan. Heat over low-medium heat, stirring occasionally, until melted and combined.

2. Increase the heat and bring just to a boil, then reduce to a low simmer and cook for 3 minutes, stirring occasionally.

3. Remove from the heat and stir in the remaining chocolate with the butter and vanilla extract. Stir until smooth and let cool slightly before transferring to jars or bottles.

4. The sauce will thicken while it cools, so before serving, reheat it in the microwave on Low for a few seconds, or in a saucepan over low heat for 30 seconds–1 minute, until still thick but pourable. Store in the refrigerator and use within 2 weeks.

CHOCOLATE MERINGUE
Kisses

Makes 40

These elegant little kisses of melt-in-the-mouth meringue dipped in chocolate make a sweet little canapé or gift.

Prep: 40 mins, plus cooling and setting   Cook: 50 mins

Ingredients

3 egg whites

1 teaspoon raspberry vinegar

¾ cup superfine sugar

1 teaspoon cornstarch

2 tablespoons unsweetened cocoa powder, sifted

8 ounces semisweet chocolate, coarsely chopped

1. Preheat the oven to 325°F. Line three baking sheets with nonstick parchment paper.

2. Whisk the egg whites in a large, clean mixing bowl until they hold stiff, moist-looking peaks. Gradually whisk in the vinegar and sugar, a tablespoon at a time, until thick and glossy. Using a large metal spoon, gently fold in the cornstarch and cocoa.

3. Spoon the meringue into a pastry bag fitted with a large star tip and pipe forty 1-inch kisses onto the prepared baking sheets.

4. Put the baking sheets into the preheated oven, then immediately reduce the oven temperature to 250°F. Bake for 45 minutes, or until crisp on the outside. Transfer the meringues to a wire rack, still on the paper, and let cool for 1 hour, then peel off the paper.

5. Meanwhile, put the chocolate in heatproof bowl set over a saucepan of gently simmering water and heat until melted.

6. Line the baking sheets with more parchment paper. Dip the bottoms of the meringue kisses into the melted chocolate and put them, chocolate side up, on the prepared baking sheets. Let set for 1 hour. Store in an airtight container in a cool, dry place for up to 2 weeks.

COMBINE

Whether you're making cakes, desserts, confectionery, or beverages, combining chocolate with well-matched ingredients makes it an even more memorable treat.

Popular combinations

Chocolate and spices

Spices and chocolate are a natural culinary match, as the Aztecs knew when they flavored their famous chocolate beverage, *xocolatl*, with chile and cinnamon.

Chocolate and chiles work well—the rich creaminess of the chocolate tempers the heat of the chile. Good-quality black pepper is another successful match. The heat stands up to the richness of chocolate, but it's subtler than chile heat. Sweet spices such as cinnamon, cardamom, and nutmeg have always been used in baking. Combined with chocolate they are even more delicious and aromatic.

Salt

Used in the correct proportion, salt balances sweet flavors. It is also an essential flavor enhancer—just a pinch will round out a cake or dessert. Salt also provides texture, and crunchy sea salt combined with semisweet chocolate is simply exquisite.

Flowers

Fragrant flowers, such as rose and lavender, combine well with semisweet chocolate. The most widely used pairing, however, is vanilla—the fermented beans of the orchid. Vanilla shows up in one form or another in most chocolate bars today.

Fruit

Chocolate and fruit is a match made in heaven, especially in cakes and desserts, as well as chocolates themselves. Dried fruits, such as golden raisins and raisins, are a classic combination, but tangy and flavorful fresh fruits tickle the taste buds, too.

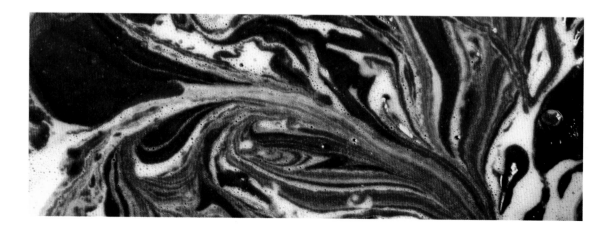

Flavor pairings table

Check the table for more details of what goes with what, and when to use it.

Ingredient		Dark Chocolate	Milk Chocolate	White Chocolate	Use
Spices	Cardamom	★ ★	★	-	Cakes, desserts, confectionery
	Chile	★ ★	★	-	Desserts, drinks, confectionery
	Cinnamon	★	★	★	Cakes, desserts, drinks, confectionery
	Ginger	★ ★	★	-	Cakes, desserts, drinks, confectionery
	Nutmeg	★	★	★	Cakes, desserts, drinks
	Pepper	★ ★	★	★	Cakes, desserts, confectionery
Salt	Sea Salt	★ ★	★	-	Cakes, desserts, confectionery
Flowers	Lavender	★	★	-	Desserts, confectionery
	Rose	★	★	-	Desserts, confectionery
	Vanilla	★ ★	★ ★	★ ★	Cakes, desserts, drinks, confectionery
Fruit	Apricots	★	★	★	Cakes, desserts, confectionery
	Bananas	★ ★	★ ★	★	Cakes, desserts, confectionery
	Cherries	★ ★	★ ★	★	Cakes, desserts, confectionery
	Lemons	★ ★	★	★ ★	Cakes, desserts, confectionery
	Limes	★ ★	-	★	Cakes, desserts, confectionery
	Oranges	★ ★	★ ★	★	Cakes, desserts, confectionery
	Pears	★ ★	★ ★	-	Cakes, desserts, confectionery
	Raisins	★	★	-	Cakes, desserts, confectionery
	Raspberries	★ ★	★ ★	★	Cakes, desserts, confectionery
	Strawberries	★	★	★	Cakes, desserts, confectionery
Herbs	Mint	★ ★	★	-	Desserts, confectionery
	Rosemary	★ ★	-	-	Desserts, confectionery
	Thyme	★	-	-	Confectionery
Nuts	Almonds	★	★	★	Cakes, desserts, confectionery
	Chestnuts	★	★	-	Cakes, desserts
	Coconut	★ ★	★ ★	★	Cakes, desserts, confectionery
	Hazelnuts	★	★	-	Cakes, desserts, confectionery
Vegetable	Beet	★	★	-	Cakes, desserts

* well paired; * * very well paired; - not reccomended

BIG CHOCOLATY
Banana Split

Makes 1

Bananas seem to have been designed to be combined with chocolate, and this old-fashioned sweet treat is still a big favorite.

Prep: 5 mins   Cook: None

Ingredients

1 large banana

2 cups chocolate ice cream

1 cup crème fraîche or whipped cream

½ cup dulce de leche (caramel sauce)

½ cup pecans, crushed

10 maraschino cherries

1. Peel and split the banana lengthwise, then put onto a rectangular serving plate.

2. Put 3 large scoops of chocolate ice cream on top of the bananas, then add the crème fraîche or whipped cream.

3. Drizzle with the dulce de leche, top with the crushed nuts and cherries, and serve immediately.

TIP
Big Banana Split just not big enough? Add scoops of vanilla ice cream and up the quantity of dulce de leche for a side-splitting banana buster.

CHOCOLATE LAVA CAKES
with Caramel Sauce

This restaurant favorite is surprisingly easy to make and can be prepared in advance. The caramel sauce makes them an extra-special indulgent treat.

Makes 10

Prep: 25 mins, plus chilling   Cook: 17–20 mins

Ingredients

1¼ sticks plus 1 tablespoon unsalted butter

4 teaspoons unsweetened cocoa powder

6 ounces semisweet chocolate, coarsely chopped

2 eggs, plus 2 egg yolks

⅔ cup superfine or granulated sugar

3 tablespoons all-purpose flour

1 tablespoon confectioners' sugar, sifted, for dusting

Caramel Sauce

4 tablespoons unsalted butter

¼ cup firmly packed light brown sugar

1 tablespoon honey

⅔ cup heavy cream

1. Melt 2 tablespoons of the butter in a small saucepan, then brush it over the insides of ten ½-cup ovenproof ramekins (individual ceramic dishes). Sift a little cocoa into each ramekin, then tilt to coat evenly, tapping out any excess.

2. Put the chocolate and the remaining butter into a heatproof bowl set over a saucepan of gently simmering water and heat, stirring occasionally, until melted.

3. Put the eggs, egg yolks, and superfine sugar into a mixing bowl and whisk together until thick and frothy and the whisk or beaters leave a trail when raised above the mixture. Sift in the flour, then gently fold it in.

4. Fold the melted chocolate mixture into the egg mixture until smooth. Pour it into the prepared ramekins, cover, and chill in the refrigerator for 1 hour, or overnight if time allows.

5. To make the caramel sauce, put the butter, sugar, and honey into a heavy saucepan and heat gently for 3–4 minutes, or until the butter has melted and the sugar dissolved, then boil for 1–2 minutes, stirring, until it begins to smell of caramel and thicken. Remove from the heat and stir in the cream.

6. Preheat the oven to 350°F. Take the ramekins out of the refrigerator and let stand at room temperature for 10 minutes. Bake in the preheated oven for 10–12 minutes, or until well risen, the tops are crusty, and the centers still slightly soft. Reheat the sauce over low heat, if needed.

7. Dust the desserts with sifted confectioners' sugar. Serve immediately with the sauce separately for pouring.

BROWN BUTTER & CHOCOLATE
Fudge Croissant Sandwiches

Makes 6

These are not your average croissants and make a wonderful weekend breakfast treat with a cup of steaming cappuccino.

Prep: 10 mins   Cook: 10 mins

Ingredients

¼ cup superfine or granulated sugar

2½ tablespoons cornstarch

1 egg

½ teaspoon vanilla extract

1 cup milk

6 store-bought croissants

⅓ cup prepared fudge sauce

2 tablespoons unsalted butter

pinch of salt

1. Whisk together the sugar, cornstarch, egg, and vanilla extract in a bowl.

2. Pour the milk into a small saucepan and bring just to a boil. Remove from the heat and pour it into the egg mixture, whisking constantly until combined.

3. Transfer to a clean saucepan, put over low heat, and heat, whisking constantly, until smooth and thick. Transfer to a bowl and cover the surface with plastic wrap to prevent a skin from forming. Let cool for 30 minutes.

4. Cut the croissants in half and spread a tablespoon of fudge sauce over the bottom half of each. Spoon the custard mixture over the fudge, then top with the remaining croissant halves.

5. Melt the butter in a large skillet over low-medium heat and add the salt. Cook for 1 minute, or until lightly browned. Add the croissants to the pan and cook for 1–1½ minutes on each side, until lightly crisped. Gently transfer the croissants to plates and serve immediately.

VARIATION
Try adding slices of
banana or strawberry
between the layers.

CHOCOLATE
Phyllo Packages

Makes 18

Phyllo pastry is a popular staple in eastern Mediterranean kitchens. These packages are filled with apples, mint, and hazelnuts for a refreshing treat.

Prep: 15–20 mins, plus cooling   Cook: 10 mins

Ingredients

½ tablespoon butter, for greasing

¾ cup ground hazelnuts

1 tablespoon finely chopped fresh mint

½ cup sour cream

2 crisp sweet apples, such as Pippin or Pink Lady, peeled and grated

2 ounces semisweet chocolate, melted

9 sheets phyllo pastry, about 6 inches square

4–6 tablespoons butter, melted

1 tablespoon confectioners' sugar, sifted, for dusting

1. Preheat the oven to 375°F. Grease a baking sheet. Mix the nuts, mint, and sour cream into a bowl. Add the apples, stir in the chocolate, and mix well.

2. Cut each pastry sheet into 4 squares. Brush a square with butter, then put a second square on top and brush with butter.

3. Put 1 tablespoon of the chocolate mixture in the center of a square, then bring up the corners and twist together. Repeat until all of the pastry and filling have been used.

4. Place the packages on the prepared baking sheet and bake in the preheated oven for about 10 minutes, until crisp and golden. Remove from the oven and let cool slightly.

5. Dust with confectioners' sugar and serve.

GOOEY CHOCOLATE
Pudding

Serves 4–6

This may be a traditional everyday dessert but our rich version is extra chocolaty and will have everyone asking for second helpings.

Prep: 5 mins, plus chilling   Cook: 25 mins

Ingredients

½ cup sugar

¼ cup unsweetened cocoa powder

2 tablespoons cornstarch

pinch of salt

1½ cups milk

1 egg, beaten

4 tablespoons butter

½ teaspoon vanilla extract

heavy cream, to serve (optional)

1. Put the sugar, cocoa powder, cornstarch, and salt into a heatproof bowl, stir, and set aside.

2. Pour the milk into a saucepan and heat over medium heat until just simmering. Do not bring to a boil.

3. Keeping the pan over medium heat, spoon a little of the simmering milk into the sugar mixture, and blend, then stir the sugar mixture into the milk in the pan. Beat in the egg and half the butter and reduce the heat to low.

4. Simmer for 5–8 minutes, stirring frequently, until the mixture thickens. Remove from the heat and add the vanilla extract and the remaining butter, stirring, until the butter is melted and has been absorbed.

5. Serve hot or chilled, with cream for pouring over the desserts, if using. If chilling the pudding, spoon it into a serving bowl, press plastic wrap onto the surface to prevent a skin from forming, and let cool completely, then chill in the refrigerator until required.

White Chocolate &
Peppermint Marshmallows

Makes 24

The traditional peppermint-and-chocolate combo is presented here in frothy, prettily decorated individual marshmallows that are just right for a party.

Prep: 45 mins, plus cooling and setting   Cook: 25 mins

Ingredients

1 tablespoon sunflower oil, for oiling

1 tablespoon cornstarch

1 tablespoon confectioners' sugar

25 large marshmallows

2–4 drops peppermint extract

4 ounces white chocolate, broken into pieces

4 small candy canes, coarsely crushed

1. Lightly oil two 12-cup silicone cupcake pans and put them onto two baking sheets. Sift together the cornstarch and confectioners' sugar into a bowl. Use a little of this mixture to lightly dust each cup.

2. Put the marshmallows into a large saucepan with a little water and heat over medium heat, stirring constantly, for 8–10 minutes, or until melted. Stir in the peppermint extract.

3. Meanwhile, put the chocolate into a heatproof bowl set over a saucepan of gently simmering water and heat until melted. Remove from the heat and stir until smooth. Let cool for 10 minutes, stirring occasionally.

4. Gently fold three-quarters of the melted chocolate into the marshmallow mixture. Spoon the mixture into the prepared pans.

5. Spoon a small swirl of the remaining melted chocolate onto each marshmallow and sprinkle with the crushed candy canes. Lightly dust the tops with a little of the coating mixture. Let set, uncovered, in a cool, dry place for 3–4 hours.

6. Carefully remove the marshmallows from the pans. Lightly dust the bottoms and sides with the remaining coating mixture. Store in an airtight container for up to 5 days.

SALTED CARAMEL
Lava Cakes

Salt and caramel have become a surprising favorite, and these little lava cakes continue the theme of the perfect duo, combining sophistication with down-to-earth flavors.

Serves 4

Prep: 20 mins   Cook: 15 mins

Ingredients

½ tablespoon butter,
for greasing

9 ounces semisweet chocolate,
chopped into chunks

1 stick butter

2 eggs, plus 2 egg yolks

½ cup superfine or
granulated sugar

¼ cup all-purpose flour

1 teaspoon sea salt flakes

¼ cup dulce de leche
(caramel sauce)

2 tablespoons unsweetened
cocoa powder, for dusting

1. Preheat the oven to 400°F. Grease four 1-cup rum baba molds. Reseve 4 chunks of the chocolate. Put the remaining chocolate into a small saucepan with the butter and heat over low heat until smooth and combined.

2. Put the eggs, egg yolks, and sugar into a large bowl and beat together until well combined. Pour the melted chocolate mixture over the egg mixture, stir to combine, then fold in the flour.

3. Fill each of the prepared molds halfway with the chocolate mixture. Mix the salt into the dulce de leche and put 1 tablespoon in the center of each mold. Top each with a chunk of the remaining chocolate. Fill the molds with the rest of the chocolate mixture to ¼ inch from the tops of the molds.

4. Place on a baking sheet and bake in the preheated oven for 16 minutes. The cakes should spring back when pressed gently. Carefully turn out the cakes and dust with the cocoa powder. Serve immediately.

VARIATION
You can swap the
dulce de leche for
peanut butter or a
chocolate spread.

REAL HOT
Chocolate

Serves 1–2

This is the perfect winter warmer. Once you've tried it, you'll probably become addicted. Top with whipped cream for a really indulgent treat.

Prep: 5 mins   Cook: 45 mins

Ingredients

1½ ounces semisweet chocolate, broken into pieces

1¼ cups milk

chocolate curls, to decorate (optional)

1. Put the chocolate into a heatproof bowl. Put the milk into a heavy saucepan and bring to a boil. Pour about one-quarter of the hot milk onto the chocolate and let stand until the chocolate is soft.

2. Whisk the milk and chocolate mixture until smooth. Return the remaining milk to the heat and bring back to a boil, then pour onto the chocolate, whisking constantly.

3. Pour into mugs or large heatproof cups and decorate with chocolate curls, if using.

FROZEN HOT CHOCOLATE
with Hazelnut Liqueur

Serves 4

Just when you thought the weather was getting too warm for hot chocolate, here is a luxurious chilled version, laced with delicious hazelnut liqueur.

Prep: 5 mins, plus cooling   Cook: 20 mins

Ingredients

3 ounces semisweet chocolate, chopped

2 tablespoons superfine sugar

1 tablespoon unsweetened cocoa powder

1½ cups skim milk

4 cups ice cubes

1 banana

¼ cup hazelnut liqueur

1. Put the chocolate into a heatproof bowl set over a saucepan of gently simmering water and heat until melted.

2. Add the sugar and cocoa powder and heat, stirring constantly, until the sugar is completely dissolved. Remove from the heat and slowly add the milk, stirring until combined. Let cool to room temperature.

3. Transfer the chocolate mixture to a blender and add the ice, banana, and hazelnut liqueur. Blend until well combined and frothy. Pour into four glasses and serve immediately.